DREAM LAUNCH GROW

A STARTUP GUIDE FOR VISIONARIES

SHIKHAR SINGH

Made with ❤ on the Notion Press Platform
www.notionpress.com

Dedication

To all the readers and viewers who dare to dream, this book is for you. Your curiosity and passion inspire innovation and creativity every day. Thank you for believing in the power of ideas and for your commitment to exploring new possibilities. May this journey guide you in your pursuit of knowledge, ignite your entrepreneurial spirit, and empower you to turn your dreams into reality. Together, let's embrace the challenges and opportunities that lie ahead, creating a future fueled by imagination and determination. Your potential knows no bounds—this book is a testament to your journey.

Contents

Preface

In the dynamic world of entrepreneurship, the journey from concept to reality is both thrilling and daunting. "Dream, Launch, Grow: A Startup Guide for Visionaries" is crafted for those who harbor bold ideas and the determination to turn them into successful ventures. Within these pages, we explore the critical strategies, insights, and lessons learned from both seasoned entrepreneurs and innovative thinkers.

This book is not just a manual; it is a roadmap for anyone who seeks to navigate the intricacies of launching a startup. From formulating a compelling vision and crafting a solid business plan to understanding the importance of sustainability and leveraging emerging technologies, we cover essential components that can shape the future of your business.

Our goal is to empower you with knowledge and confidence, dispelling the myth that entrepreneurship is solely for a select few. We believe that anyone with passion and perseverance can achieve their dreams. Throughout the chapters, you'll find practical advice, inspiring stories, and actionable steps tailored to guide you on your unique journey.

As you embark on this adventure, remember that every successful entrepreneur started with a dream. This book aims to ignite your vision, provide clarity in the launch phase, and support your growth as you navigate the exciting challenges ahead. Let's turn those dreams into reality together.

Welcome to your entrepreneurial journey.

CHAPTER ONE

The Visionary Mindset

The Visionary Mindset

The visionary mindset is the cornerstone of entrepreneurial success. It is defined by the ability to see beyond the present, innovate, and inspire others. In this chapter, we will explore the essential elements of the visionary mindset, highlighting the differences between visionaries and traditional entrepreneurs, cultivating creative thinking, overcoming fear and self-doubt, developing a clear vision and mission, and understanding the importance of passion in entrepreneurship.

1. The Difference Between a Visionary and an Entrepreneur

While the terms "visionary" and "entrepreneur" are often used interchangeably, there are distinct differences between the two.

Entrepreneur: An entrepreneur is primarily someone who identifies a business opportunity and takes on the risks involved in creating a business to exploit that opportunity. Entrepreneurs are usually more focused on the operational aspects of their ventures—they concern themselves with business models, marketing strategies, and financial management. They often seek to solve a specific problem and establish a profitable entity.

Visionary: In contrast, visionaries have a broader conceptualization of their role. They are not only focused on the immediate business opportunities but also on the long-term impact of their ideas. Visionaries are often future-oriented, able to articulate what the future could look like based on their insights and passions. They inspire others to share in their vision and may work in various capacities, including social innovation, cultural movements, and community-building projects. Visionaries often see trends before they become evident to others, leveraging their insights to influence change.

The key distinction lies in the scope of their focus: entrepreneurs drive businesses, while visionaries drive change. Visionaries ask "What if?" and challenge the norm, leading not just with numbers and business plans but with a compelling narrative that can rally people around a cause.

2. Cultivating Creative Thinking

Creative thinking is essential for both entrepreneurs and visionaries. However, visionaries need to cultivate this skill deliberately, as it enables them to generate innovative ideas and solutions. Here are methods to enhance creative thinking:

1. Embrace Curiosity: Visionaries must maintain a sense of curiosity. By questioning assumptions and exploring varied perspectives, they can generate novel ideas and identify hidden opportunities. Keeping a journal for ideas, reflections, or insights can help maintain a steady stream of creativity.

2. Practice Divergent Thinking: Divergent thinking is the ability to generate multiple solutions to a problem. Brainstorming sessions where no idea is dismissed, along with techniques like mind mapping, encourage diverse thinking that leads to unexpected results.

3. Foster a Creative Environment: Surround yourself with people who inspire you. Engage with a diverse group of thinkers and creatives to stimulate your imagination. Participation in workshops, seminars, and discussions can lead to cross-pollination of ideas.

4. Allow for Play: Engaging in creative activities without the pressure of producing a finalized product can foster innovation. Activities such as drawing, writing, or even role-playing can unlock your nervous inhibitions, allowing your mind to wander and create freely.

5. Create Time for Reflection: In our fast-paced world, reflection is often overlooked. Taking time to ponder ideas, re-evaluate plans, and incorporate feedback can bring clarity to scattered thoughts and spark new insights.

By deliberately cultivating creative thinking, visionaries refine their ability to brainstorm, innovate, and motivate others to think outside the box. This skill is not merely advantageous; it is essential for realizing their potential impact on the world.

3. Overcoming Fear and Self-Doubt

Fear and self-doubt are common challenges that anyone with a vision might face. The prospect of failure, judgment, or a lack of support can stall even the most brilliant of ideas. Overcoming these obstacles requires conscious effort and resilience.

1. Acknowledge Your Fears: The first step to overcoming fear is to acknowledge and understand it. Take time to reflect on what specifically instills fear—whether it's the fear of failure, rejection, or inadequacy. Understanding the roots of your anxiety allows you to devise strategies to combat them.

2. Reframe Negative Thoughts: It's essential to challenge negative narratives that arise from self-doubt. Instead of thinking, "What if I fail?", reframe this thought to "What can I learn from this experience?" This simple shift in perspective can motivate you to see obstacles as opportunities for growth.

3. Set Achievable Goals: Break down your larger goals into smaller, actionable steps. Completing these steps provides a sense of accomplishment and builds confidence. Celebrate small victories, as they will reinforce your belief in your vision.

4. Surround Yourself with Support: A support network can play a crucial role in overcoming fear. Seek mentors, advisors, or peers who can provide encouragement and constructive criticism. Surrounding yourself with successful and positive individuals can naturally uplift your spirits.

5. Embrace Failure as a Teacher: Reframe your perception of failure. Instead of viewing it as a finite end, see it as an invaluable teacher. Studying what went wrong and how you can improve fosters resilience and prepares you for future endeavors.

While fear and self-doubt are inevitable, a visionary can develop strategies to overcome them. By doing so, they not only propel themselves forward but also become a source of inspiration for others facing similar challenges.

4. Developing a Clear Vision and Mission

A clear vision and mission are pivotal for any visionary. They act as the North Star guiding decisions and strategies toward long-term objectives. Below are steps to develop a compelling vision and mission:

1. Defining Your Core Values: Values dictate the foundation of your vision. Identify what principles are non-negotiable for you and your startup. These values will guide every decision, shaping company culture and establishing its identity in the marketplace.

2. Envisioning the Future: Spend time visualizing what success looks like for your venture. Where do you see your business in five or ten years? Articulate a vision statement that encapsulates this aspirational future. Ensure it's specific enough to provide direction but broad enough to allow for growth.

3. Crafting a Mission Statement: A mission statement is actionable and represents the purpose of your startup. It should outline what you do, whom you serve, and how you intend to serve them. An effective mission statement distills the essence of your vision into clear, actionable terms.

4. Communicating Your Vision and Mission: Once defined, it's crucial to communicate this vision and mission consistently across all platforms and among stakeholders—including employees, investors, and customers. Everyone should understand the shared goals and motivations.

5. Reviewing and Revising: Your vision and mission should not be static. As your business evolves, so will your vision. Regularly review and adjust as necessary. Remain receptive to new ideas while ensuring they align with your core values and overarching mission.

A strong vision and mission provide a roadmap for navigating challenges and create a sense of unity among team members. They serve both as a guide and as a motivational rallying point for achieving long-range goals.

5. The Importance of Passion in Entrepreneurship

Passion is arguably one of the most critical qualities that can drive a visionary entrepreneur's success. It fuels persistence, attracts talent, and fosters innovation. Below, we explore the facets of passion and its significance in entrepreneurship:

1. Driving Motivation: Passion is the force that propels visionaries toward their goals, even in the face of challenges. It instills a sense of purpose, making difficult tasks seem manageable and worthwhile. Passionate entrepreneurs are more likely to put in the long hours required to bring their visions to fruition.

2. Inspiring Others: A strong sense of passion is infectious. When visionaries are enthusiastic about their ideas, they inspire those around them—whether they are team members, investors, or customers. Effective leaders harness this energy to create a motivated and engaged workforce, fostering a positive company culture.

3. Fueling Innovation: Passionate individuals are more likely to explore new ideas and challenge the status quo. This exploration leads to innovation and creativity, pushing boundaries and creating products or services that are disruptive and transformative.

4. Resilience in Adversity: Entrepreneurship is replete with highs and lows. Passion provides the resilience necessary to navigate turbulent times. When faced with setbacks, a passionate entrepreneur is more likely to persist, learning and adapting rather than giving up.

5. Aligning with Purpose: Passion ensures that your work aligns with your values and interests. When you are emotionally invested in what you are doing, fulfillment and satisfaction often follow. This alignment creates a holistic experience where work is not merely a job, but a meaningful endeavor.

Undoubtedly, passion is a critical element of success in entrepreneurship. It serves as the foundation for motivation, inspires teams, fuels innovation, fosters resilience, and aligns one's work with personal values. In cultivating a visionary mindset, embracing passion is a vital step that empowers individuals to not just dream, but to launch and grow their startups.

Conclusion

The visionary mindset encapsulates essential traits and skills necessary for turning dreams into reality. Understanding the differences between visionaries and entrepreneurs, cultivating creative thinking, overcoming fear, establishing a clear vision and mission, and nurturing passion are all integral components. By embracing these elements, aspiring visionaries can navigate the complexities of entrepreneurship and drive meaningful change in their ventures and beyond.

This chapter not only sets the stage for further exploration into the startup journey but also ignites the potential within each reader to become a catalyst for transformative ideas and impactful enterprises.

CHAPTER TWO

Identifying Your Unique Idea

Identifying Your Unique Idea

Identifying a unique business idea is arguably one of the most critical steps in the entrepreneurial journey. It requires creativity, market understanding, and validation to ensure that what you envision can become a viable business. In this chapter, we delve into five essential components of identifying your unique idea, covering brainstorming techniques, identifying market gaps, validating ideas, researching competitive landscapes, and defining your unique selling proposition (USP).

1. Brainstorming Techniques for Idea Generation

Brainstorming serves as the foundation for generating new business ideas. It's a creative process that encourages free thinking and the generation of a wide array of ideas. Here are several effective brainstorming techniques:

a. Mind Mapping: This technique involves writing down a central idea and branching out into related ideas. For example, if you're interested in technology, you might start with "tech innovations" and branch into subcategories like "wearables," "smart home devices," or "health tech." Mind mapping helps visualize relationships and foster new connections between ideas.

b. Reverse Brainstorming: Instead of thinking about how to solve a problem, consider how to create one. For instance, if you want to develop a product that helps people stay organized, brainstorm ways to make people more disorganized. This technique often uncovers hidden insights and can lead to unexpected solutions.

c. Brainwriting: In this method, participants write down their ideas on paper, then pass the paper around for others to add their thoughts. This can be particularly effective for reducing the pressure on individuals to come up with the "perfect" idea in a verbal group setting, allowing for deeper collaboration and refinement of concepts.

d. SCAMPER: This technique stands for Substitute, Combine, Adapt, Modify, Put to another use, Eliminate, and Reverse. It prompts you to think critically about existing products or services and how they can be improved or transformed. For example, consider how a successful app could be adapted for a different audience or how two distinct products could be combined to create something new.

e. Customer Feedback Sessions: Engaging directly with potential customers can provide rich insights. Ask targeted questions about their frustrations or desires related to certain products or services. This not only generates ideas but also lays the groundwork for understanding what lives in your customers' minds.

Using a combination of these brainstorming techniques can foster creative discussions and help generate a myriad of ideas. The key is to remain open-minded and avoid self-editing during the initial idea phase; allow thoughts to flow freely before narrowing them down.

2. Identifying Market Gaps and Opportunities

Once you have a pool of ideas, the next step is to analyze the market to identify gaps and opportunities. A market gap refers to an area where consumer needs are not fully met, presenting an opportunity for new products or services.

a. Conduct Market Research: Utilizing surveys, focus groups, and interviews helps gather insights about consumer preferences and pain points. Create questionnaires to determine what customers value most, what challenges they face, or what features they wish existed in current offerings.

b. Analyze Trends: Keep an eye on industry trends, technological advancements, and socio-economic factors that might influence consumer behavior. Tools like Google Trends, social media insights, and market reports can provide valuable data. For example, you might notice a growing interest in eco-friendly products, indicating a market need.

c. Create Customer Personas: Building detailed profiles of your target customers can help pinpoint gaps. Identify demographics, interests, and purchasing behaviors. With this information, tailor your offerings to meet the specific needs and desires of your target market.

d. Evaluate Existing Solutions: Study competitors' products or services. Analyze customer reviews and ratings to discover what users like or dislike about these offerings. If you can identify consistently unaddressed pain points, you could have found a promising market gap.

e. Leverage Your Skills and Passions: Reflect on your own experiences, expertise, and interests. Often, the best business ideas come from personal frustrations or observations. If something has frustrated you or your peers, it may have broader implications for the market.

Identifying market gaps requires a blend of data analysis and emotional intelligence. Your observations can lead you to discover unfilled niches that may not be immediately obvious.

3. Validating Your Business Idea

Validation is crucial to ensuring that your idea has the potential to succeed in the marketplace. A validated idea gives you confidence that your business will attract customers and generate profit. Here are key steps to validate your business idea:

a. Create a Prototype or MVP: Developing a Minimum Viable Product (MVP) allows you to test your idea without extensive investment. An MVP incorporates only the essential features of your product. For instance, if you're creating a mobile app, draft the core functionalities needed to deliver the primary value proposition.

b. Conduct User Testing: Share your MVP with a select group of potential users. Gather feedback through surveys or interviews about their experience using the product. What did they find helpful? What challenges did they encounter? User testing provides invaluable insights into the usability and relevance of your solution.

c. Launch a Landing Page: A simple landing page can help gauge interest in your idea. Include details about your concept and a call to action, such as signing up for a newsletter. Monitor how many visitors convert into leads; this indicates potential market interest.

d. Reach Out to Your Network: Discuss your idea with trusted friends, mentors, or industry professionals. Their feedback can offer different perspectives. If possible, aim to find someone with experience in your chosen field.

e. Use Crowdfunding Platforms: Launching a campaign on platforms like Kickstarter or Indiegogo can act as both a validation and a funding opportunity. A successful campaign indicates that there is market demand for your idea, while also helping you raise valuable funds.

Validating your business idea ensures that you invest time and resources into something with a solid market foundation. It opens up the opportunity to pivot your approach based on real feedback.

4. Researching Competitive Landscapes

Understanding your competition is essential for positioning your startup effectively. Competitive analysis involves both direct and indirect competitors and helps you develop strategies to differentiate your offering.

a. Identify Direct and Indirect Competitors: Direct competitors offer similar products or services targeting the same audience. Indirect competitors may fulfill a similar need but offer different solutions. Categorizing competitors helps you understand the broader landscape.

b. SWOT Analysis: Conduct a SWOT (Strengths, Weaknesses, Opportunities, Threats) analysis for key competitors. This involves evaluating their market positioning, customer base, revenue, product offerings, and marketing strategies. Such assessment can illuminate where you could excel or face challenges.

c. Analyze Their Marketing Strategies: Investigate how competitors reach and communicate with their customers. Assess their content strategies, social media presence, and advertising approaches. This can inform your own marketing plan and highlight gaps in their messaging you could exploit.

d. Study Customer Reviews and Feedback: Customer feedback on products or services often reveals opportunities for differentiation. Pay attention to common complaints or praises; this insight can guide you to refine your offerings.

e. Use Competitive Analysis Tools: Various online tools, such as SEMrush, SpyFu, or Ahrefs, allow you to analyze competitors' traffic sources, keywords, and backlinks. This data is instrumental for understanding their marketing tactics and online presence.

By thoroughly researching the competitive landscape, you can discover unique angles to position your business. This knowledge is pivotal in defining your unique selling proposition (USP).

5. Defining Your Unique Selling Proposition (USP)

A unique selling proposition (USP) is the clear and compelling reason why customers should choose your product or service over another. Your USP articulates the value you provide that differentiates you in the marketplace.

a. Highlight Your Benefits: Start by identifying the core benefits of your product or service. What specific problems does it solve, and what advantages do customers gain? For example, if your product reduces energy costs, it's worth emphasizing both the financial savings and the environmental impact.

b. Focus on What Sets You Apart: Reflect on the insights gained from your competitive analysis. What unique features or capabilities does your business possess that competitors lack? This could be anything from exceptional customer service to innovative technology or unique product design.

c. Emphasize Your Target Audience: Clarify who your ideal customer is and how your offering speaks directly to their needs. Personalization can make your USP more compelling. For instance, if your product is eco-friendly, marketing it to environmentally-conscious consumers strengthens your message.

d. Articulate Your Message Clearly: Craft a concise and memorable statement that encapsulates your USP. This statement should be simple enough for anyone to understand and remember. For example, FedEx's "When it absolutely, positively has to be there overnight" communicates a compelling promise to customers.

e. Test Your USP: Once defined, test your USP with your target audience. Are they receptive to your message? Does it resonate? Gathering feedback will help refine your positioning and ensure your USP aligns with consumer expectations.

Developing a strong USP is crucial for attracting customers and establishing brand loyalty. It sets the foundation for your marketing strategy and communication.

Conclusion

Identifying your unique business idea involves creative brainstorming, understanding market needs, validating your concept, analyzing competition, and defining your unique selling proposition. Each step builds upon the previous one, allowing for the development of a comprehensive strategy that aligns creativity with market realities.

By effectively navigating these components, you lay a strong foundation for your startup, ultimately enabling you to convert your vision into a thriving business. The entrepreneurial journey is challenging, but by focusing on these critical elements, you can pave the way for success and innovation in your chosen market segment.

CHAPTER THREE

Crafting a Business Plan

Crafting a Business Plan

Creating a business plan is one of the most essential steps in launching and managing a startup. A comprehensive business plan serves not only as a roadmap for your business but also as a tool for communicating your vision to potential investors, partners, and stakeholders. In this chapter, we'll discuss the key components of a business plan, the importance of goal-setting, financial projections, marketing strategies, and evaluating possible business models.

1. The Components of a Comprehensive Business Plan

A well-structured business plan typically includes several key components that provide a holistic view of your business. Here are the essential elements:

1. Executive Summary:

The executive summary is a brief overview of your business, usually one to two pages long. It should succinctly summarize your business idea, mission statement, and the problem your startup aims to solve. Also, include your business model, target market, and how you plan to succeed. This section is crucial as it sets the tone for the rest of the document and helps investors quickly understand your vision.

2. Company Description:

This section provides an in-depth view of your business, including its name, location, legal structure (e.g., LLC, corporation), and core values. Discuss what makes your business unique and what problems it aims to address. Include details about your industry, your business's history (if applicable), and your long-term objectives.

3. Market Analysis:

Conducting thorough market research is vital. This section should include an analysis of your target market, demographics, market size, and trends. Additionally, evaluate your competitors by analyzing their strengths and weaknesses. This information not only demonstrates your awareness of the market landscape but also helps you identify your competitive advantage.

4. Organization and Management:

This part outlines your business's organizational structure. Include information about the ownership (founders, investors), key team members, and their roles and responsibilities. You can also include an organizational chart to visualize your business hierarchy. Highlight the skills and experiences of your management team to instill confidence in your potential investors.

5. Products or Services Offered:

Detail what you are selling or the services you are providing. Explain how your offerings meet the needs of your target market and outline any unique features or advantages. If applicable, discuss your pricing strategy, the stages of product development, and any plans for future product lines or services.

6. Marketing and Sales Strategy:

In this section, specify how you plan to attract and retain customers. Discuss your promotional strategies, channels, and sales process. Highlight any marketing techniques, such as social media marketing, content marketing, or SEO, that you plan to employ to reach your audience.

7. Funding Request:

If you are seeking funding, this section is vital. Clearly articulate how much capital you need, how you will use the funds, and the preferred terms of investment or lending. This is your opportunity to outline any specific investment opportunities, such as equity stakes or loans.

8. Financial Projections:

This part includes projected income statements, cash flow statements, and balance sheets for the next three to five years. Financial projections lend credibility to your business plan, so it's crucial to provide realistic and well-researched figures that demonstrate potential profitability and financial sustainability.

9. Appendix:

An appendix can include supplementary information such as resumes, legal agreements, product images, or additional market research. This section allows you to present documents that provide additional context without cluttering the main body of the plan.

2. Setting Short-Term and Long-Term Goals

Setting goals is fundamental to any startup's success. Clear goals provide direction and benchmarks for progress. Understanding the difference between short-term and long-term goals is crucial to effective business planning.

1. Defining Short-Term Goals:

Short-term goals typically span from a few weeks to a year. These goals should be specific, measurable, achievable, relevant, and time-bound (SMART). Examples of short-term goals may include:

- Completing market research within three months.
- Launching a website in 6 weeks.
- Securing your first ten customers within six months.

2. Importance of Short-Term Goals:

Short-term goals help maintain focus and motivation. Achieving these smaller objectives creates momentum and encourages your team to stay engaged. They also facilitate ongoing assessments, allowing you to make necessary adjustments to your strategies.

3. Establishing Long-Term Goals:

Long-term goals focus on objectives that fall several years into the future—generally three to five years. These could include expanding into new markets, achieving a specific revenue target, or developing a new product line.

4. Aligning Short- and Long-Term Goals:

Both types of goals should align with your overall vision. Long-term goals should inform your short-term objectives, ensuring that each small achievement acts as a stepping stone toward your larger ambitions.

5. Regular Review and Adjustment:

It's essential to regularly review both short-term and long-term goals. As your business environment changes, you may need to adapt your objectives to stay relevant and successful. Regular assessments help ensure that your business remains on track toward achieving its vision.

3. Financial Projections and Funding Needs

Understanding your financial needs and providing accurate projections is critical for attracting investors and managing your business effectively.

1. Importance of Financial Projections:

Financial projections estimations about future revenue, expenses, and profits. They demonstrate to investors that you have a robust understanding of your financial landscape and can articulate sound growth strategies.

2. Creating Pro Forma Financial Statements:

Include at least three types of financial statements in your projections:

- **Income Statement:** It shows revenues, expenses, and profit over a specific period. This statement gives insights into operational efficiency and profitability.
- **Cash Flow Statement:** It tracks the cash inflows and outflows, helping you ensure you have enough liquidity to meet your obligations. Positive cash flow is crucial for long-term sustainability.
- **Balance Sheet:** This outlines your assets, liabilities, and equity. It provides an overview of your company's financial position at a specific point in time.

3. Funding Requirements:

Be clear about your funding needs, including total capital required and how those funds will be allocated. Common funding needs include:

- Startup costs such as equipment, inventory, and renovations.
- Operating expenses including salaries, rent, and utilities.
- Marketing expenses to promote your brand and attract customers.
- Research and development costs for product development.

4. Financing Options:

Discuss the different financing avenues available to your startup, like venture capital, angel investors, bank loans, or crowdfunding. Each option has advantages and drawbacks, so it's essential to choose based on your business model and long-term goals.

5. Milestones and Metrics:

Connect your financial projections to key milestones. Define metrics you will use to measure progress, such as customer acquisition costs, lifetime value of a customer, or gross profit margins. This approach helps you monitor and adjust your strategies effectively.

4. Outlining Marketing Strategies

Marketing strategies dictate how you promote your offerings and attract customers. A well-defined marketing plan is essential for building brand awareness and driving sales.

1. Identifying Your Target Audience:
Begin by clearly defining your target audience. Understand their demographics, preferences, and behaviors. Use tools like customer personas to create a comprehensive profile of your ideal customers.

2. Choosing Marketing Channels:
Select marketing channels where your audience is most active. Common channels include:

- **Social Media:** Platforms like Facebook, Instagram, and LinkedIn allow you to connect with your audience effectively.
- **Content Marketing:** Developing valuable content (blogs, videos, infographics) positions you as an authority in your field.
- **Email Marketing:** Sending newsletters and promotional emails can drive engagement and conversions.

3. Developing a Unique Value Proposition (UVP):
Your UVP communicates what makes your offerings different and better than competitors. It should be clear, concise, and resonate with your target audience. Use your UVP in your marketing messaging to reinforce your brand's value.

4. Creating a Marketing Budget:
Outline your marketing budget, detailing expenses for each channel and initiative. Allocate resources strategically to ensure a balanced approach that maximizes return on investment.

5. Measuring Effectiveness:
Use analytics tools to track the performance of your marketing campaigns. Monitoring metrics such as website traffic, conversion rates, and customer engagement will help you assess effectiveness and refine your strategies.

5. Evaluating Possible Business Models

Understanding and evaluating various business models can greatly influence your startup's success. A business model outlines how your company creates, delivers, and captures value.

1. Types of Business Models:
Explore different business models commonly used in startups:

- **B2C (Business to Consumer):** Direct sales to consumers, commonly seen in retail.
- **B2B (Business to Business):** Providing products or services to other businesses.
- **Subscription Model:** Charging customers a recurring fee for ongoing access to a product or service (e.g., SaaS).
- **Freemium Model:** Offering a basic product for free while charging for premium features.

2. Strengths and Weaknesses:
Evaluate the strengths and weaknesses of potential business models in relation to your startup. Consider factors such as market size, competition, and customer behavior. This analysis can highlight which model might best meet your business objectives.

3. The Importance of Flexibility:
Your chosen business model should reflect your startup's unique strengths and fit the market needs. However, be open to adapting your model as your business evolves. Many successful companies pivoted their models based on customer feedback and market dynamics.

4. Revenue Streams:
Identify your revenue streams early on. Understand how different models might influence your pricing strategy, sales volume, and overall revenue potential. Assessing diverse revenue streams can also help in mitigating risks.

5. Market Fit:
A great business model should find a fit with its market. This involves understanding customer pain points and ensuring that your offerings address them effectively. Continually test assumptions and be willing to pivot if your hypothesis doesn't align with market realities.

Conclusion

Crafting a business plan is a vital step for any aspiring entrepreneur. By focusing on the key components of the plan, setting actionable goals, projecting finances, outlining effective marketing strategies, and evaluating viable business models, you lay a solid foundation for your startup's success. Remember, a business plan is a living document that should be revisited and adjusted regularly as your business grows and market conditions change.

Embrace the journey, adapt to challenges, and stay committed to your vision as you navigate the entrepreneurial path.

This comprehensive look at crafting a business plan provides insights and strategies necessary for startups to envision their road ahead while aligning their goals with actionable steps.

CHAPTER FOUR

Building Your Brand

Building Your Brand

1. Understanding Brand Identity and Values

Definition and Importance

Brand identity is the collection of elements that a company creates to portray the right image to its consumer. It includes your company's logo, color palette, typography, and overall design elements, but it goes far beyond mere aesthetics. At its core, brand identity encompasses how your audience perceives your business and differentiates it from competitors.

Your brand values are the beliefs and principles that guide your business's actions. They set the foundation for your brand identity. When well articulated, brand values resonate with your target audience, fostering loyalty and trust.

Components of Brand Identity

1. **Logo**: This is the graphic representation of your brand. It is often the first element that people associate with your company. A successful logo is memorable, versatile, and can convey meaning without words.
2. **Color Palette**: Colors evoke emotions and reactions. Different colors can influence how customers perceive your brand. Choosing a suitable color palette is crucial. For instance, green often symbolizes sustainability, while blue can evoke feelings of trust.
3. **Typography**: The font you choose communicates your brand's personality. A modern sans-serif font might suggest innovation and forward-thinking, while a serif font might convey tradition and reliability.
4. **Imagery and Graphics**: This includes the kind of images, icons, and graphics you use in your marketing materials. Consistency in imagery helps reinforce your brand identity.

Creating Brand Values

Define your core values by considering what truly matters to your business. Ask yourself:

- Why did you start this company?
- What principles do you want to stand for?
- How do you want your customers to feel after interacting with your brand?

Creating a list of 3-5 core values can help you stay aligned with your mission.

Putting It All Together

Once you have clarity on your brand identity and values, document them in a brand guideline. This document will serve as a roadmap for all branding efforts moving forward, ensuring consistency across all touchpoints.

2. Designing Your Logo and Visual Elements

The Role of Your Logo

Your logo is often the face of your brand. It's the first impression customers will have, making it crucial for this element to capture the essence of your business. A well-designed logo should be simple, memorable, and capable of scaling across various mediums.

Logo Design Process

1. **Research:** Look into competitors to understand common themes in your industry. This will help you identify what works and ensure your logo stands out.

2. **Conceptualize:** Brainstorm ideas that encapsulate your brand's values. Sketch out various concepts, focusing on how these ideas reflect what your brand stands for.

3. **Design and Iterate:** Utilize graphic design software like Adobe Illustrator to create digital versions of your logo. Experiment with different fonts, color combinations, and layouts.

4. **Seek Feedback:** Once you have a few concepts, gather feedback from potential customers, friends, or design communities. Take this feedback into account for further refinements.

5. **Finalize:** Choose a logo that resonates with your target audience and meets design objectives. Prepare multiple versions and file types for use across different platforms.

Visual Elements Beyond the Logo

Design is not just about the logo; it's about creating a cohesive visual identity. Here are additional elements to consider:

- **Business Cards**: Essential for networking, your business card should encapsulate your logo and key brand colors while providing clear contact information.
- **Marketing Materials**: Flyers, brochures, and promotional items should maintain consistent branding, utilizing the same typography and color scheme.
- **Packaging**: If you're selling products, investing in high-quality packaging that reflects your brand identity can enhance customer experience.

Importance of Consistency

Consistency is key in building brand awareness. Use the same logo, color palette, and typography across all platforms—online and offline. Inconsistencies can confuse customers and dilute your brand identity.

3. Developing Your Brand Voice and Messaging

What is Brand Voice?

Brand voice refers to the tone and style of how a company communicates with its audience. It's a crucial aspect of brand identity, as it affects how customers perceive your brand. A well-defined brand voice fosters connection and engagement, allowing your audience to relate to your message.

Components of Brand Voice

1. **Tone**: The attitude expressed in your messaging—formal, casual, humorous, etc. A startup in tech might adopt a friendly, conversational tone, while a legal firm might opt for a more serious tone.
2. **Language**: The choice of words you use can also convey your brand's identity. Avoid jargon unless it's appropriate for your audience. Be mindful of complexity versus simplicity based on your target customers.
3. **Pacing**: The speed of your messaging delivery can influence impressions. Short, snappy sentences can convey excitement, while longer, detailed explanations may indicate thoroughness.

Crafting Your Messaging Strategy

1. **Define Your Audience**: Understand who your target customers are. Knowing their preferences, challenges, and desires will help tailor your brand voice effectively.
2. **Align with Brand Values**: Ensure your brand voice reflects your core values. A brand emphasizing sustainability should communicate in an environmentally friendly manner.
3. **Create Messaging Guidelines**: Document your brand voice in a style guide. This guide should contain examples of dos and don'ts for internal and external communication.

Implementing Brand Messaging

Create targeted messaging for different platforms—your website, social media, email newsletters, etc. Ensure that the messaging aligns with the context and resonates with the audience of each platform.

4. Creating an Effective Website

The Importance of Your Website

Your website is often the first point of contact for potential customers. An effective website functions as your digital storefront—a place where users can learn about your brand, explore your products or services, and take action, such as making a purchase or signing up for a newsletter.

Key Elements to Include

1. **User-Friendly Navigation**: A clean and intuitive layout enhances the user experience. Ensure that visitors can find information swiftly, with clear headings and logical menu items.
2. **Responsive Design**: With increasing mobile traffic, your site must be optimized for different devices. A responsive design automatically adjusts to fit screens of tablets, smartphones, and desktops.
3. **Compelling Content**: High-quality content that provides value keeps visitors engaged. Use clear headlines, persuasive copy, and captivating images to create a seamless reading experience.
4. **Calls to Action (CTA)**: CTAs guide visitors to the next steps—be it signing up for a newsletter, making a purchase, or contacting you. Use prominent and persuasive language to encourage clicks.
5. **SEO Optimization**: Optimize your website for search engines by using relevant keywords, meta tags, and alt text for images. This will increase your website's visibility and attract organic traffic.

Additional Considerations

- **Load Speed**: Ensure your site loads quickly; delays can lead to increased bounce rates. Use tools like Google PageSpeed Insights to monitor and optimize performance.
- **Security**: Protect customer information by investing in security measures like SSL certificates, which create secure connections.
- **Analytics**: Implement tools like Google Analytics to track user behavior on your website. Analyze metrics such as page views, bounce rates, and conversion rates to make data-driven improvements.

5. Establishing Your Online Presence via Social Media

The Importance of Social Media

Social media platforms provide invaluable opportunities for businesses to connect with their audience, promote their products, and nurture customer relationships. With billions of users globally, social media is an effective marketing tool that can amplify your brand message.

Choosing the Right Platforms

1. **Identify Your Audience**: Understanding your target market is crucial to selecting the platforms where they spend their time. For example, younger audiences may prefer Instagram or TikTok, while professionals may lean towards LinkedIn.
2. **Align Platforms with Brand Goals**: Different platforms serve various purposes. Instagram is visual; LinkedIn is professional. Choose platforms that align with your brand strategy and audience behavior.

Creating Engaging Content

1. **Content Types**: Experiment with various content formats—images, videos, stories, live streams, and polls—to keep your audience engaged.
2. **Consistency**: Regularly update your social media profiles to keep the audience engaged. Develop a content calendar outlining what you will post and when.
3. **Community Engagement**: Respond to comments and messages promptly. Engage your audience through interactive content, such as polls or contests, to foster a sense of community.

Monitoring Performance

Utilize analytics tools provided by social media platforms (e.g., Facebook Insights or Instagram Analytics) to measure performance. Track engagement rates, follower growth, and post reach to evaluate the effectiveness of your strategies.

Conclusion

Building a brand is a multifaceted process that requires careful consideration of your identity, visual elements, messaging, online presence, and more. A strong brand sets the foundation for customer loyalty and long-term success. By delving into these key components, you can create a cohesive and compelling brand that resonates with your audience and stands the test of time. Your brand is more than just your product; it embodies your vision, values, and interactions with the world. Invest time and effort in building it right, and your startup has a greater chance of achieving its long-term goals.

This breakdown serves as both a foundation and an actionable guide for brand building, emphasizing the importance of a cohesive approach at all steps. Each section emphasizes actionable strategies designed to foster a coherent and distinctive brand presence that attracts and retains customers.

CHAPTER FIVE

Assembling Your Team

Assembling Your Team

Building a startup from the ground up is an exhilarating journey filled with possibilities, yet it can also be fraught with challenges. One of the most critical components determining the success of your venture is the team you assemble. This chapter provides a deep dive into the essentials of assembling a high-performing team, covering key roles, recruitment strategies, team culture, diversity and inclusion, and effective training and onboarding processes.

1. Identifying the Key Roles Needed for Your Startup

When launching a startup, it's important to identify the roles that are essential for your business's success. Each role should be aligned with your startup's mission and operations. Here are key roles that most startups should consider:

- **Founder(s):** As the visionary behind the idea, founders are typically responsible for shaping the company's direction and culture. They often handle initial fundraising efforts, customer outreach, and strategic decisions.
- **Chief Executive Officer (CEO):** In some cases, the founder acts as the CEO. This role involves overseeing the company's operations, setting strategic goals, and ensuring that the organization works toward its vision effectively.
- **Chief Operating Officer (COO):** The COO manages day-to-day operations, ensuring efficient processes align with business objectives. They work closely with department heads to implement strategies and drive growth.

- **Chief Financial Officer (CFO):** The finance lead oversees budgeting, forecasting, and financial strategy, ensuring the company has the resources it needs to achieve its goals while managing risks effectively.
- **Product Manager:** This role revolves around developing the product vision and strategy. Product managers gather user feedback, collaborate with engineering and design teams, and prioritize features based on market demand.
- **Marketing Manager:** Responsible for crafting marketing strategies to promote the product, the marketing manager will focus on understanding the target audience, developing campaigns, and measuring their effectiveness.
- **Sales Team:** Comprising sales representatives and account managers, this team is tasked with driving revenue by attracting new clients and maintaining relationships with existing customers.
- **Customer Support Representatives:** These individuals are the first line of communication with customers. They handle inquiries, resolve issues, and ensure customer satisfaction.
- **Technical Team:** Depending on the nature of your startup, you may need software developers, engineers, or designers to bring your product or service to life. This team is responsible for the technical aspects and should be aligned with product goals.

The composition of your team may evolve as your startup grows and the market changes. It's crucial to remain flexible and reassess your team's needs regularly to ensure you have the right people in the right roles.

2. Recruitment Strategies to Attract Talent

Once you've identified the key roles needed for your startup, the next step is recruiting talent who not only have the necessary skills but also fit your startup's culture and vision. Here are effective recruitment strategies:

- **Develop a Compelling Employer Brand:** Articulate your startup's mission, vision, and values in a way that resonates with potential candidates. Showcase your company culture through social media, your website, and employee testimonials.
- **Leverage Networking:** Utilize your professional network to spread the word about open positions. Attend industry events, career fairs, and meetups where you can meet potential candidates face-to-face.

- **Use Job Boards and Platforms Wisely:** Post your job openings on platforms like LinkedIn, Glassdoor, and specialized job boards relevant to your industry. Tailor your job descriptions to attract the right candidates.
- **Implement an Employee Referral Program:** Encourage your current employees to refer candidates from their networks by offering incentives for successful hires. This often leads to high-quality applications, as referred candidates usually align closely with the startup's culture.
- **Engage with Universities and Alumni Associations:** Partner with local universities to tap into fresh talent. Participate in career fairs and internships, mentoring students, and building relationships that could lead to future hiring opportunities.
- **Conduct Comprehensive Hiring Processes:** Ensure you have a structured hiring process that includes multiple interview rounds, and assessments, and reflects on cultural fit. Involve team members in the hiring process to ensure cohesive collaboration.
- **Showcase Growth Opportunities:** Talented individuals often seek roles that offer opportunities for advancement. Communicate clear paths for professional development within your organization, including mentorship, training programs, and leadership roles.

By employing these strategies, you can attract top talent that shares your vision for the startup and is eager to contribute to its growth.

3. Building a Culture of Collaboration and Innovation

A startup's culture significantly influences team dynamics and productivity. Fostering a culture of collaboration and innovation can help your team thrive. Here are methods to build this culture:

- **Encourage Open Communication:** Create an environment where team members feel comfortable sharing ideas, asking questions, and providing feedback. Utilize tools like Slack or Microsoft Teams to facilitate quick communication.
- **Promote Inclusivity:** Ensure that every team member feels valued and heard. Celebrate diverse perspectives, and actively seek input from all employees when making decisions, fostering a sense of ownership across the organization.
- **Invest in Team-Building Activities:** Organize regular team-building exercises to strengthen interpersonal relationships. Activities can

include collaborative projects, team outings, or workshops that allow employees to bond outside of work tasks.

- **Celebrate Failures and Successes:** A culture that embraces experimentation encourages innovation. Celebrate both achievements and lessons learned from failures, creating a safe space for taking calculated risks.
- **Create a Flexible Work Environment:** Offer flexibility in work hours and remote work options to improve work-life balance. When employees feel their personal needs are respected, they are likely to be more engaged and productive.
- **Set Innovation Goals:** Establish specific goals relating to innovation, such as implementing a certain number of new ideas per quarter. This encourages an ongoing pursuit of creativity among team members.

A culture that prioritizes collaboration and innovation can lead to higher employee morale, improved productivity, and enhanced creativity, ultimately driving the startup forward.

4. The Importance of Diversity and Inclusion

Diversity and inclusion (D&I) are not just moral imperatives; they are business advantages that can lead to increased creativity, innovation, and problem-solving capabilities within your team. Here are reasons to prioritize D&I in your startup:

- **Broader Perspectives:** A diverse team brings together individuals from varied backgrounds, experiences, and viewpoints. This diversity results in a wider range of ideas and solutions, which is critical for innovation.
- **Enhanced Employee Engagement:** When employees see themselves represented within the organization and feel included in decision-making processes, their morale and commitment increase, leading to a more motivated workforce.
- **Improved Customer Understanding:** A diverse team can better understand and connect with a wide range of customers. This helps create products and services that resonate deeply with various demographics, expanding your market reach.
- **Stronger Problem-Solving Abilities:** Diverse teams often outperform homogenous ones in problem-solving scenarios. This is because differing perspectives encourage creative thinking and innovation, enabling teams to tackle challenges more effectively.

- **Attracting Top Talent:** Many candidates seek employers committed to D&I. Building an inclusive workplace can attract high-quality talent and help your startup stand out in a crowded job market.

To foster D&I in your startup, start by establishing D&I goals and holding regular training sessions. Develop policies that promote equal opportunities and seek diverse candidates during recruitment.

5. Training and Onboarding for New Team Members

Effective training and onboarding are essential for setting new hires up for success. A well-structured onboarding process can lead to lower turnover rates and higher job satisfaction. Here are steps to create an effective training and onboarding program:

- **Develop an Onboarding Plan:** Outline the key stages of onboarding, including introductions to team members, training schedules, and performance expectations. A structured plan helps new hires navigate their first few weeks confidently.
- **Assign a Mentor or Buddy:** Pair new hires with a mentor or buddy who can guide them through the onboarding process and answer questions. This personal support can help them acclimate to the company culture and foster connections.
- **Provide Comprehensive Training:** Identify key competencies required for the new role and offer appropriate training resources. This could be through workshops, online courses, or hands-on training from existing team members.
- **Establish Clear Performance Metrics:** Communicate performance expectations from the outset. Set measurable goals for new hires, and regularly check in to provide feedback and support, allowing them to learn and adapt.
- **Solicit Feedback:** After onboarding, ask new hires for their feedback on the process. Understanding their experience can inform improvements to make onboarding more effective and welcoming for future recruits.
- **Encourage Continuous Learning:** After the initial onboarding phase, continue to invest in employee development through ongoing training programs, workshops, and access to resources that encourage skill enhancement.

A robust training and onboarding process not only equips new team members with the skills they need but also fosters a sense of belonging and community within the startup.

Conclusion

Assembling a talented and diverse team is crucial for the success of any startup. By identifying key roles, implementing strategic recruitment tactics, fostering a culture of collaboration and inclusion, and investing in effective training and onboarding, you lay a strong foundation for your organization. A well-rounded and united team not only drives innovation but also ensures that your vision is realized, propelling your startup toward sustainable growth and success. The journey may be challenging, but the rewards of building and nurturing a capable team are immeasurable.

CHAPTER SIX

Funding Your Dream

Funding Your Dream: A Comprehensive Guide

Securing funding is often one of the most critical steps for startups. Without sufficient capital, even the most innovative ideas can falter. In this section, we will explore various funding options available for aspiring entrepreneurs, discuss how to craft an effective pitch deck, compare different types of investors, delve into crowdfunding, and analyze the financial metrics that can influence funding decisions.

1. Exploring Different Funding Options

Bootstrapping Bootstrapping refers to the practice of self-funding a startup through personal savings, revenue generated by the business, or reinvested profits. This method allows entrepreneurs to retain full control of their company without giving away equity or incurring debt. Some benefits of bootstrapping include:

- **Ownership**: Full control over business decisions and direction.
- **Flexibility**: Ability to pivot and adapt without having to seek approval from investors.
- **Validation**: Building a business with minimal funding can signal to future investors that the concept is viable.

However, bootstrapping can be challenging as it limits initial growth and can lead to financial strain. Entrepreneurs must balance expenses while seeking to grow their business.

Angel Investors Angel investors are individuals who provide capital in exchange for ownership equity or convertible debt. These investors often have a high-risk tolerance and are motivated by the potential for significant returns. Securing funding from angel investors can provide valuable resources beyond capital, such as networking opportunities and mentorship. When approaching angel investors, it is crucial to present a clear business plan and a defined exit strategy, as they will want to understand how they will make a return on their investment.

Venture Capitalists (VCs) Venture capitalists are professional investment firms or funds that invest in high-growth startups in exchange for equity. VCs typically look for businesses that demonstrate significant market potential and scalability. The funding process usually involves several stages, including:

- **Initial Research**: VCs will assess the industry and market trends.
- **Due Diligence**: A thorough examination of the business plan, financial statements, and market position.
- **Term Sheet Negotiation**: Outlining the terms of investment, including ownership percentage, board seats, and exit plans.

While venture capital can accelerate growth, it is essential for entrepreneurs to understand the terms of engagement, as they involve relinquishing a degree of control and ownership.

Loans Loans can be obtained from traditional banks or alternative lenders and can take various forms, such as personal loans, business loans, or lines of credit. Here are some key considerations regarding loans:

- **Collateral**: Many lenders require collateral, which could put personal or business assets at risk.
- **Repayment Terms**: Understanding the terms and interest rates associated with any loan is crucial.
- **Creditworthiness**: A strong credit score often plays a significant role in loan approval.

Loans can provide a necessary source of funding and allow entrepreneurs to maintain ownership, but they also come with an obligation to repay, regardless of business success.

Grants and Competitions Startup grants are often provided by governments, nonprofit organizations, or private entities to fund new businesses in specific industries or areas of innovation. Some competitions also offer cash prizes as well as resources to help early-stage entrepreneurs. These can be particularly appealing since they do not require repayment. However, competition for grants can be fierce, and applicants must demonstrate a clear need for the funding and how it will be utilized.

2. Crafting a Compelling Pitch Deck

A pitch deck is a visual presentation that outlines the key aspects of your business and serves as a gateway to getting funding. A well-structured pitch deck typically includes the following elements:

Problem Statement Clearly define the problem your startup is addressing. Use real-world examples or anecdotes to illustrate the pain points experienced by your target market. This helps investors understand the significance of the issue.

Solution Present your product or service as the solution to the problem you've identified. Explain how it works and the tangible benefits it provides. This section should also highlight what makes your solution unique compared to existing alternatives.

Market Opportunity Identify the target market and provide data to support its size, potential for growth, and your anticipated market share. Include statistics, charts, and market trends to strengthen your argument.

Business Model Detail how your startup plans to make money. This could include pricing strategy, sales channels, and customer acquisition methods. Clearly state your revenue streams, which can include online sales, subscriptions, licensing, etc.

Traction and Milestones Showcase any traction your startup has already achieved. Whether it's user growth, revenue, partnerships, or product development milestones, this evidence demonstrates the viability of your business and its potential for future success.

Marketing Strategy Outline how you plan to reach and acquire customers. Discuss your marketing channels, sales strategies, and how you intend to leverage social media, content marketing, or public relations.

Financial Projections Provide realistic financial forecasts that cover at least three to five years. Include expected revenue, costs, profits, and potential funding requirements. This information allows investors to understand your financial outlook and the scalability of your business.

Team Highlight the backgrounds and expertise of your founding team. Showcase essential qualifications, experiences, and any previous successes in entrepreneurship. Investors invest in people as much as they invest in ideas.

Call to Action Conclude the pitch deck with a clear request for funding and specify how you plan to use the investment. Whether it's for product development, marketing, or hiring new staff, providing clarity helps potential investors understand the impact of their investment.

By crafting a compelling pitch deck, startups can effectively communicate their vision, ignite interest, and differentiate themselves from competitors.

3. Approaching Venture Capitalists vs. Angel Investors

While both venture capitalists and angel investors provide funding to startups, their motivations, investment strategies, and the stages at which they typically invest can differ significantly.

Angel Investors

- **Investment Size**: Typically invest smaller amounts, often between $25,000 to $500,000.
- **Stage**: Usually invest in early-stage companies or startups, often before they have a fully developed product or significant traction.
- **Involvement**: Often take a hands-on approach and may provide mentorship or guidance alongside capital.
- **Evaluation Criteria**: May consider personal connection with entrepreneurs and be more open to risk, largely driven by passion for the idea.

When determining whether to approach an angel investor, startups should focus on building personal relationships and demonstrating passion and commitment to their vision.

Venture Capitalists

- **Investment Size**: Invest larger sums of money, often ranging from $1 million to several million.
- **Stage**: VCs typically look for companies that have already established a product in the market and have shown some degree of success in traction.
- **Involvement**: Usually take a more hands-off approach, although they may require board positions to influence strategic decisions.
- **Evaluation Criteria**: Focus on scalability, market potential, existing traction, and financial metrics. VCs also conduct extensive due diligence before investing.

Given these differences, startups must tailor their approach based on the type of investor they aim to attract.

4. Crowdfunding Strategies and Platforms

Crowdfunding is an increasingly popular method for startups to raise funds by collecting small amounts of money from a large number of people, typically through online platforms. Below are some effective strategies for raising funds through crowdfunding:

Choose the Right Platform There are several crowdfunding platforms, each catering to different types of projects. Popular platforms include:

- **Kickstarter**: Best for creative projects and products. Offers all-or-nothing funding where projects must reach their goals to receive funds.
- **Indiegogo**: More flexible than Kickstarter, supporting a wider range of projects, including personal and charitable causes.
- **GoFundMe**: Primarily used for personal fundraising, but also supports entrepreneurial endeavors.

Set Clear Goals and Rewards Establish a clear funding goal that reflects your financial needs. Offering rewards can incentivize backers to contribute; these can include early access to products, branded merchandise, or exclusive updates. Make sure the rewards correspond with the donation levels to enhance the appeal.

Develop an Engaging Campaign Craft a compelling narrative surrounding your startup. Utilize a combination of storytelling, visuals, and videos to convey your idea, mission, and the difference it seeks to make. Authenticity is crucial here; engage with your audience on a personal level.

Leverage Social Media Promoting your crowdfunding campaign on social media can significantly broaden your reach. Use platforms such as Facebook, Twitter, and Instagram to share updates and personal stories, encouraging your followers to support your project and share it with their networks.

Maintain Communication and Updates Maintain regular communication with backers throughout your campaign. Provide updates on progress, share stories, and express gratitude. This builds a sense of community and keeps supporters informed and engaged.

Crowdfunding can provide significant exposure, validation, and capital for startups, but it requires careful planning and execution.

5. Understanding the Financial Metrics Investors Look For

When seeking funding, it's essential for entrepreneurs to understand the financial metrics that investors consider when assessing the viability of a startup.

Monthly Recurring Revenue (MRR) For subscription-based businesses, MRR is a key metric that provides insight into revenue consistency. Growth in MRR indicates a healthy, scalable business model. Investors will often look for a steady increase in MRR over time, showcasing customer retention and acquisition strategies' effectiveness.

Customer Acquisition Cost (CAC) CAC measures the costs involved in acquiring new customers. It includes marketing expenses, salespeople salaries, and other associated costs. Investors seek a low CAC, which signifies efficient marketing and sales efforts. Comparing CAC to customer lifetime value (CLV) will provide investors with insights into profitability and growth strategies.

Customer Lifetime Value (CLV) CLV estimates the total revenue an average customer will generate over their relationship with the business. A high CLV compared to CAC signifies a healthy business model, as it indicates that acquiring customers is not only manageable but also lucrative in the long run.

Burn Rate Burn rate is the rate at which a startup is losing cash relative to its revenue. Understanding this metric helps investors assess how long a startup can operate before needing additional funding. A lower burn rate relative to MRR is usually favorable.

Runway Runway calculates the time a startup has left before it runs out of cash. This is determined by dividing current cash reserves by the burn rate. Investors prefer startups with a longer runway, as they indicate sufficient time to reach key milestones or secure additional funding.

In conclusion, understanding these funding mechanisms and what investors look for enables entrepreneurs to navigate the complex financing landscape effectively. By exploring various options, presenting compelling business cases, and being adept with financial metrics, startups can increase their chances of securing the necessary funding to bring their visions to life.

CHAPTER SEVEN

Launching Your Startup

Launching Your Startup

Launching a startup is a pivotal moment that can determine its future success. Preparation, strategy, and execution play critical roles in how effectively you can introduce your product or service to the market. Below, we'll explore five essential topics for a successful startup launch.

1. Setting a Launch Date and Timeline

Establishing the Right Timing

Choosing a launch date is a strategic decision that requires careful consideration of multiple factors. A well-thought-out timeline reflects not just readiness but targets the best possible window for market entry. Here are important aspects to consider when setting your launch date:

- **Market Readiness:** Evaluate industry trends, your competitors' activities, and potential market demands. Sometimes, it makes sense to wait for a particular event or season to maximize visibility.
- **Product Readiness:** Ensure your product or service is ready for public use. This means not only having a functioning product but also being prepared with quality support systems and marketing materials.
- **Team Availability:** Align your launch timeframe with your team's workload and availability. Overextending your team can lead to burnout, errors, and ultimately, a less effective launch.
- **Stakeholder Input:** Gather insights from your advisors, mentors, and investors. Their experience can provide additional perspectives on market timing that you may have overlooked.

Creating a Timeline

Once the launch date is set, create a timeline that outlines key milestones leading up to the launch. This timeline should include:

- **Pre-Launch Activities**: Schedule activities that build excitement, such as content releases, beta testing, partnerships, and promotional campaigns.
- **Marketing Initiatives**: Plan your marketing strategies weeks or even months in advance. This could involve digital marketing, PR outreach, social media strategies, or community events.
- **Launch Day Preparations**: Outline specific tasks for the launch day, including team responsibilities, customer engagement strategies, and social media activity.
- **Post-Launch Follow-Up**: Develop a plan for following up after the launch, which may include additional marketing efforts, feedback collection, and customer engagement strategies.

Setting a launch date and a detailed timeline helps align your efforts, making the launch process smoother and more focused.

2. Pre-Launch Marketing: Building Buzz and Anticipation

The Importance of Pre-Launch Marketing

Pre-launch marketing plays a critical role in generating excitement and anticipation among potential customers. Building buzz before the launch can significantly improve initial traction and sales.

Strategies for Building Buzz

- **Teaser Campaigns**: Create curiosity by releasing sneak peeks of your product. This could include short videos, behind-the-scenes content, or glimpses of features that will be available at launch.
- **Build an Email List**: Open a pre-launch email signup page that offers potential customers exclusive access or discounts on the launch day. Use landing pages, social media promotions, and partnerships to entice users to sign up.
- **Engage with Influencers**: Collaborate with influencers or thought leaders in your industry. Send them free samples or beta versions of your product in exchange for honest reviews or shoutouts on their social media platforms.
- **Leverage Social Media**: Utilize platforms such as Instagram, Twitter, LinkedIn, and Facebook to engage your audience. Regularly post content that showcases the benefits of your product, shares your story, and keeps followers updated on launch preparations.
- **Content Marketing**: Start a blog or video series to discuss your industry, your journey, and the problems your product solves. This positions you

as a thought leader and provides value to potential customers.

- **Run Contests and Giveaways**: Organize contests where participants need to follow your social media and share your content. This can increase your reach and engagement while creating excitement around your launch.

Measuring Buzz Levels

Track your pre-launch marketing effectiveness through analytics. Monitor your website traffic, email signups, social media engagement, and mentions to understand how well you're resonating with your audience and to refine strategies as necessary.

3. Developing a Minimum Viable Product (MVP)

Understanding the MVP Concept

A Minimum Viable Product (MVP) is a product version with just enough features to satisfy early adopters and collect feedback for future development. The idea of an MVP is to avoid investing significant resources into full scale product development before validating your concept.

Steps to Develop an MVP

- **Identify Core Features**: Determine which features are critical for your product to serve its basic function. Focus on solving the primary pain points of your target audience.
- **Create User Stories**: Employ user stories to articulate how your product will be used. This will guide your development efforts, ensuring that each feature delivers value to the end user.
- **Prototyping and Design**: Use wireframes or prototypes to visualize your product. Tools like Sketch, Figma, or Adobe XD allow you to create preliminary designs that can guide development.
- **Develop and Test**: Build the MVP using an agile approach, allowing for iterative testing and improvements based on user feedback. Aim for a functional product with the capacity for future enhancements.
- **Feedback Loop**: Launch the MVP to a select group of users (beta testers) and collect feedback. Analyze their experiences, preferences, and suggestions for improvements.

The Value of an MVP

Developing an MVP reduces the risks associated with product launch. It allows you to validate your business model, test assumptions, and make data-driven decisions for future development. As you gather feedback, you can better understand customer needs and pivot or refine your product accordingly.

4. Conducting a Successful Launch Event

The Role of the Launch Event

A launch event serves as a focal point for your marketing efforts, creating a memorable moment that celebrates your startup and announces its entrance into the market. A well-executed event can enhance brand visibility, attract media attention, and create an opportunity for direct engagement with customers.

Steps to Plan a Successful Launch Event

- **Define Your Goals**: Determine what you hope to achieve with your launch event. Goals may include acquiring customers, gaining press coverage, or simply building community excitement.
- **Choose the Right Venue**: Depending on your audience size and preferences, select a physical location or consider a virtual event format. Ensure the venue aligns with your brand image and is suitable for the type of experience you want to create.
- **Create an Engaging Agenda**: Plan an event agenda that includes a combination of presentations, demonstrations, and interactive sessions. Consider including guest speakers, panel discussions, or live demonstrations to maintain audience interest.
- **Promote the Event**: Use your marketing channels to publicize the event. Share details through social media, email newsletters, and your website. Partner with local influencers or media outlets to extend outreach.
- **Coordinate Logistics**: Ensure all logistical aspects are handled meticulously, such as catering, technology (AV setup), seating arrangements, and materials (brochures, swag bags).

Post-Event Engagement

Following the event, take time to analyze its success. Gather feedback from attendees to assess what worked well and what could be improved for future events. Share video highlights, photos, and messages on your social channels to maintain the momentum and engagement you've built.

5. Collecting Early Feedback to Iterate and Improve

The Importance of Feedback

Early feedback is essential for iterative improvement, providing insights into how your product is received and areas for enhancement. Feedback loops allow you to refine your product, ensuring it meets customer needs and expectations.

Methods for Collecting Feedback

- **Surveys and Questionnaires**: Deploy post-launch surveys to gather structured feedback. Include questions regarding usability, functionality, and overall satisfaction. Tools like Google Forms or Typeform can facilitate this.
- **User Testing Sessions**: Conduct user testing sessions where participants engage with your product while you observe their interactions. This provides invaluable insights into user behavior and pain points.
- **Social Media Engagement**: Use your social media platforms to solicit feedback. Encourage users to share their thoughts, either through direct messages, comments, or by tagging your business in posts.
- **Customer Support Channels**: Monitor customer support inquiries closely to identify recurring issues or questions. This can reveal areas where the product may not be clear or intuitive.
- **Focus Groups**: Assemble small focus groups made up of target customers to discuss their experiences with the product. This qualitative feedback can provide deeper insights into customer perceptions.

Implementing Feedback for Improvement

Once feedback is collected, prioritize changes based on the frequency and severity of the issues raised. Create a roadmap that outlines how you will address these concerns in future updates or iterations of your product. Communicate transparently with your users about the changes based on their feedback, reinforcing their role in your development process.

Conclusion

Successfully launching a startup involves detailed planning, strategic marketing, product development, event organization, and constructive feedback cycles. Each of these critical components contributes to building a strong foundation for your business, ensuring that it resonates with the market and has the best chance of thriving. By approaching your launch with a clear strategy and a focus on customer engagement, you position your startup for long-term success.

CHAPTER EIGHT

Marketing Strategies for Startups

Marketing Strategies for Startups
1. Traditional vs. Digital Marketing: What's Right for You?
Understanding Traditional Marketing:

Traditional marketing refers to the conventional methods of promoting products and services, which have been employed for decades. This includes print advertisements, television and radio ads, direct mail, billboards, and in-person events like trade shows. The advantages of traditional marketing lie in its ability to reach a broad audience quickly and its established practices that resonate with certain demographics, particularly older consumers who may not be as active online.

- **Advantages:**

  - **Wider Reach:** Traditional media, especially television, can reach millions of viewers at once. This is advantageous for launches or announcements.
  - **Tangible Presence:** Billboards and flyers are hard to ignore; their physical presence can create lasting impressions.
  - **Trust Factor:** Many consumers trust traditional media more than digital channels, as they perceive these to be well-regulated and credible.

- **Disadvantages:**

  - **Costly:** Advertising spaces such as television or radio slots can be expensive, making it difficult for startups to enter the market.

- ○ **Difficulty in Targeting:** Traditional marketing often casts a wide net, making it challenging to target niche demographics efficiently.

Understanding Digital Marketing:

Digital marketing leverages online platforms, including social media, search engines, websites, and email to reach consumers. This type of marketing has emerged recently and is characterized by its cost-effectiveness, measurable outcomes, and real-time interaction capabilities.

- **Advantages:**

  - ○ **Targeted Approach:** Digital marketing allows startups to target specific audiences based on demographics, behavior, and interests, effectively maximizing marketing spend.
  - ○ **Cost-Effective:** Many digital marketing strategies, like social media marketing and email campaigns, can be executed at a fraction of the cost of traditional markcting.
  - ○ **Measurable Results:** Digital tools provide access to analytics that help measure the effectiveness of campaigns in real time, allowing businesses to adjust their strategies promptly.

- **Disadvantages:**

  - ○ **Information Overload:** With the sheer volume of online content, startups may struggle to capture their audience's attention.
  - ○ **Constantly Evolving:** Digital marketing trends change rapidly, which may require continuous learning and adaptation.

Choosing the Right Approach:

The decision between traditional and digital marketing should be based on your target audience, budget, and the nature of your startup. For example, a local restaurant may benefit more from traditional methods like local newspapers and flyers, while a tech startup targeting younger consumers would find greater success through social media and search engine marketing. Many startups find value in a hybrid approach that combines both strategies to maximize reach and effectiveness.

2. Content Marketing and its Benefits

What is Content Marketing?

Content marketing is a strategic marketing approach focused on creating and distributing valuable, relevant content to attract and engage a clearly defined audience. The goal is to drive profitable customer action by building trust and rapport through consistent, quality content.

Types of Content Marketing:

- **Blog Posts:** Informative articles that provide value to readers while improving search engine rankings.
- **Videos:** Engaging visual content can convey complex information quickly while appealing to emotional responses.
- **Infographics:** Graphical representations of information that can simplify complex data for easily digestible understanding.
- **Podcasts:** Audio content that allows in-depth discussions on relevant topics, showcasing expertise and building a loyal audience.
- **Whitepapers and Ebooks:** In-depth studies on topics relevant to your industry that can position your startup as a thought leader.

Benefits of Content Marketing:

- **Builds Brand Authority:** By consistently delivering valuable content, startups can establish themselves as experts in their field, fostering trust among potential customers.
- **Improves SEO:** Quality content can improve organic search rankings by incorporating relevant keywords, enhancing visibility and driving traffic to your website.
- **Engages Your Audience:** Quality content facilitates communication with customers, encouraging feedback and interaction. Engaged audiences are more likely to convert into paying customers.
- **Generates Leads:** Effective content marketing drives higher-quality leads through gated content (like ebooks) that require an email signup, fostering a direct line of communication.
- **Cost-Effective Long-Term Strategy:** While initial content creation costs may be high, its longevity creates a lasting impact that can continue to attract leads long after publishing.

Developing a Content Marketing Strategy:
To implement content marketing effectively, startups should:

- Define their target audience and create content that specifically addresses their pain points or interests.
- Create a content calendar to maintain consistency and align content with business goals and audience needs.
- Utilize various formats and channels to reach a diverse audience (i.e., social media, email, and blogs).
- Measure the impact of content through various metrics like website traffic, engagement, and lead generation rates, adjusting strategies as necessary.

3. Social Media Strategies to Grow Your Audience
Understanding Social Media Marketing:
Social media marketing involves using social platforms to connect with your audience, improve brand awareness, and drive website traffic. Popular platforms include Facebook, Instagram, Twitter, LinkedIn, and TikTok, each serving different demographics and purposes.
Creating a Social Media Strategy:

1. **Identify Your Audience:** Understanding your target demographic will help you determine which platforms to focus on. Different age groups and interests prefer different platforms.
2. **Set Clear Objectives:** Define what you want to accomplish (e.g., increasing brand awareness, driving traffic, generating leads). Each goal requires different tactics.
3. **Develop Engaging Content:** Create a mix of content types, including promotional posts, behind-the-scenes snippets, customer testimonials, informative content, and interactive posts (like polls or Q&As). Visual elements also enhance engagement.
4. **Consistency is Key:** Regularly posting content keeps your audience engaged. Use editorial calendars to plan and schedule content in advance.
5. **Utilize Influencer Marketing:** Collaborating with influencers can expand your reach significantly. Identify influencers within your niche who resonate with your target audience.

Measuring Success:
Monitor engagement metrics such as likes, shares, comments, click-through rates, and follower growth. Utilize platform-specific analytics tools

or third-party tools to gauge the effectiveness of different content types and campaigns. Adjust your strategy based on what performs well.

4. Search Engine Optimization (SEO) Basics for Startups

What is SEO?

Search Engine Optimization (SEO) is the practice of optimizing your online content to ensure that it is more visible in search engine rankings. The goal is to drive organic (non-paid) traffic to your website by improving your position in search results.

Key Components of SEO:

1. **Keyword Research:** Identify and utilize keywords that your target audience is searching for. Use tools like Google Keyword Planner, SEMrush, or Ahrefs to find relevant keywords.
2. **On-Page SEO:** This includes optimizing various elements on your website, such as titles, headings, meta descriptions, and content quality to align with targeted keywords. It also involves ensuring your website is user-friendly and mobile-responsive.
3. **Technical SEO:** Focuses on the technical aspects of your website, including site speed, secure connections (HTTPS), XML sitemaps, and ensuring your website is indexable by search engines.
4. **Off-Page SEO:** This refers to building your website's authority through backlinks from other reputable websites, social media engagement, and local SEO efforts (like Google My Business for local startups).
5. **Content Quality:** Producing quality, engaging content that addresses user search intent is critical to driving organic traffic. Content should be well-researched, informative, and updated regularly.

Measuring SEO Effectiveness:

Use tools like Google Analytics and Google Search Console to track organic traffic, keyword rankings, and other important metrics. Look for trends and insights that can guide your content strategy and SEO improvements.

5. Measuring Marketing Metrics and KPIs

Understanding Marketing Metrics and KPIs:

Marketing metrics are quantifiable measures that assess the performance of marketing activities. Key Performance Indicators (KPIs) are specific metrics that reflect the success of a campaign in relation to established objectives.

Key Metrics to Measure:

1. **Traffic Metrics:**

   - **Website Traffic:** Total visits to your website in a specific period.
   - **Traffic Sources:** Breakdown of where traffic is coming from (organic search, social media, direct visits, referrals).

2. **Engagement Metrics:**

   - **Bounce Rate:** Percentage of visitors who leave after viewing only one page. A high bounce rate may indicate that the content is unsatisfactory or irrelevant.
   - **Average Session Duration:** Measures how long visitors stay on your site. Longer durations often reflect engaging content.

3. **Conversion Metrics:**

   - **Conversion Rate:** Percentage of visitors who complete a desired action (such as filling out a form, making a purchase, or signing up for a newsletter).
   - **Cost Per Acquisition (CPA):** Total marketing spend divided by the number of new customers acquired.

4. **Email Marketing Metrics:**

   - **Open Rate:** Percentage of recipients who open your email. This metric indicates how compelling your subject line is.
   - **Click-Through Rate (CTR):** Percentage of recipients who clicked on one or more links within the email, reflecting the effectiveness of the email content.

5. **Social Media Metrics:**

   - **Engagement Rate:** Measures the interaction of followers with posts (likes, shares, comments), reflecting how well your content resonates.

- ○ **Follower Growth Rate:** Tracks how your social media following increases over time, indicative of brand awareness and outreach.

Adjusting Strategies:

Regularly analyzing these metrics will inform your overall marketing strategy, allowing you to identify what works and what doesn't. Use this data to make informed adjustments to your campaigns and initiatives, optimizing for better results.

Conclusion

In the competitive landscape of startups, effective marketing strategies are essential to build brand awareness and achieve business growth. Emerging entrepreneurs must carefully navigate the options available to them, employing a mix of traditional and digital marketing, leveraging the power of content, engaging audiences through social media, optimizing for search engines, and continually measuring their effectiveness through relevant metrics. By doing so, they can successfully transform their vision into a thriving business.

Sales Techniques for New Businesses

Sales Techniques for New Businesses

Effective sales techniques are essential for the success of any startup. In this chapter, we will explore vital components to develop your sales strategy, foster customer relationships, create a cohesive sales process, leverage technology for sales management, and master closing techniques. Let's dive into each topic in detail.

1. Developing a Sales Strategy for Your Startup

A well-defined sales strategy serves as the roadmap for your sales efforts. It aligns your business goals with actionable steps and outlines how you will reach and engage potential customers. Here's how to develop an effective sales strategy:

a. Define Your Target Market: Understanding exactly who your ideal customers are is crucial. Segment your market based on demographics (age, gender, location), psychographics (values, interests), and behaviors (buying patterns, usage rates). Create detailed buyer personas that encapsulate these characteristics, which will guide your outreach and messaging.

b. Set Clear Sales Goals: Establishing measurable and achievable sales goals is fundamental. Use the SMART criteria—Specific, Measurable, Achievable, Relevant, Time-bound. For example, instead of a vague goal like "increase sales," set a goal to "increase sales by 20% in the next quarter through targeted email campaigns."

c. Analyze the Competition: Conduct a comprehensive analysis of your competitors. Understand their offerings, pricing strategies, strengths, and weaknesses. This information will help you find ways to differentiate your products and services in your sales strategy.

d. Develop Your Unique Value Proposition (UVP): What makes your product unique? Your UVP should clearly convey to potential customers the specific benefits and value they will receive from your offering. This statement should be concise and focus on how your solution addresses their pain points better than competitors.

e. Choose Your Sales Channels: Determine the best channels to reach your target audience. Depending on your business model, this may include direct sales, online sales, partnerships, or distributors. Each channel will necessitate different approaches, so tailor your sales strategy accordingly.

f. Create a Sales Process: Outline clear steps in your sales process—from lead generation to closing the deal. Establish stages, such as initial contact, needs assessment, proposal, negotiation, and closing. This structured approach will help streamline your sales efforts and make it easier to track progress.

A well-developed sales strategy provides clarity and direction, ensuring that your sales team remains focused on efforts that will drive growth for your startup.

2. Building Relationships with Prospective Clients

Establishing meaningful relationships with prospects is a cornerstone of successful sales. The ability to connect with your audience fosters trust, opens lines of communication, and significantly increases your chances of closing sales. Here's how to build those critical relationships:

a. Personalize Communications: Personalization goes beyond addressing your prospects by name. Reference their specific needs, interests, and pain points in your communications. Demonstrating that you understand their unique situation can significantly increase engagement. Use CRM tools to track interactions and tailor your messages accordingly.

b. Active Listening: Listen to your prospects more than you speak. Encourage them to share their thoughts, challenges, and goals. By understanding them deeply, you can offer tailored solutions that resonate, reiterating the value you bring. Active listening shows you value their input and establishes a foundation for a long-term relationship.

c. Follow-Up Strategically: Many sales happen after multiple touchpoints; do not hesitate to follow up. However, ensure that your follow-ups are meaningful. Recap previous discussions, share relevant content, or simply check in to see how they are doing. Consistent yet thoughtful follow-up reinforces your dedication and keeps your offering top-of-mind.

d. Offer Value Before Asking: Instead of immediately pitching your product, focus on providing value upfront. Share industry insights, helpful resources, or advice related to their challenges. By positioning yourself as a knowledgeable partner rather than just a seller, you create goodwill and trust, paving the way for future sales.

e. Utilize Social Selling: Leverage social media platforms such as LinkedIn, Twitter, or Facebook to engage with prospects. Join relevant groups, participate in discussions, and share valuable content that aligns with their interests. By adding value within these social spaces, you can build your reputation and nurture relationships organically.

Building strong relationships requires patience and genuine effort. When prospects feel valued, they are more likely to trust you with their business, leading to increased sales and long-term loyalty.

3. Creating a Sales Funnel and Customer Journey

A well-designed sales funnel guides prospects through their buying journey from discovery to purchase. Understanding this journey allows you to engage with prospects at each stage effectively. Here's how to create and manage your sales funnel:

a. Map the Customer Journey: Start by identifying the key stages in your customer journey: Awareness, Consideration, Decision, and Post-Purchase. Consider what information or support a prospect needs at each stage. For instance, in the Awareness stage, they might seek educational content, while in the Decision stage, they may require detailed product information and comparisons.

b. Develop Marketing Material for Each Stage: Create tailored content that aligns with each stage of the funnel. For example, informative blog posts and social media posts can introduce potential customers to your brand in the Awareness stage, while case studies or product demos can facilitate decision-making in the Decision stage.

c. Use Lead Magnets: Encourage prospects to enter your sales funnel by offering valuable lead magnets—this could be an eBook, free trial, webinar, or exclusive content. Collect their contact information in exchange for the lead magnet, allowing you to nurture them through email marketing or retargeting efforts.

d. Implement an Email Nurturing Campaign: Once leads enter your funnel, engage with them regularly through email. Segment your audience based on their stage in the funnel and personalize your emails accordingly. Provide relevant content, insights, and calls to action that move them closer to a purchase decision.

e. Analyze and Optimize the Funnel: Employ analytics tools to track metrics such as conversion rates at each stage of your funnel. Identify any bottlenecks, such as high drop-off rates in certain phases, and refine your strategies to improve overall funnel performance. Continuous optimization ensures that your sales process remains efficient and effective.

Creating a structured sales funnel clarifies the customer journey and gives you tools to engage effectively at every stage of their decision-making process.

4. Leveraging CRM Tools for Sales Management

Customer Relationship Management (CRM) tools are indispensable for managing interactions with prospects and customers. They provide valuable insights and streamline various sales processes. Here's how to effectively leverage CRM tools:

a. Choose the Right CRM Software: Research and select a CRM platform that aligns with your startup's needs and budget. Popular options include Salesforce, HubSpot, and Zoho. Look for features such as contact management, lead tracking, reporting, and integrations with other tools you use.

b. Centralize Customer Data: Use your CRM to store all relevant customer data—contact information, interaction history, and notes from meetings or calls. Having a centralized database ensures your sales team has easy access to the information needed to engage effectively.

c. Automate Repetitive Tasks: Leverage CRM automation features to reduce manual tasks. Automate follow-up emails, reminders for calls, and data entry to allow your sales team to focus on more strategic activities. This can boost productivity and improve response times to prospects.

d. Analyze Sales Performance: Use your CRM's reporting capabilities to monitor sales performance metrics such as conversion rates, sales cycle length, and revenue generated. Regular analysis can help identify top-performing strategies and areas needing improvement, guiding future sales efforts.

e. Facilitate Collaboration: Encourage your sales team to use the CRM collaboratively. Share notes, insights, and updates about prospects' needs within the platform. A collaborative environment fosters teamwork and ensures everyone is aligned toward closing deals.

Utilizing CRM tools not only organizes your sales process but enhances communication and collaboration among team members, ultimately leading to more effective customer engagements.

5. Closing Techniques: Turning Leads into Customers

Mastering closing techniques is integral to converting leads into paying customers. While each prospect is unique, there are several proven strategies that can help increase your closing rates:

a. Recognize Buying Signals: Pay attention to verbal and non-verbal cues that indicate readiness to buy. This could include asking specific questions about product details, comparing options, or expressing urgency. Responding promptly to these signals can capitalize on their enthusiasm, leading to successful closures.

b. Use the Assumptive Close: The assumptive close is when you act as if the prospect has already made the decision to purchase. For instance, you might say, "When would you like us to deliver the product?" This technique can create a sense of normalcy around making a purchase, easing any hesitations.

c. Present Limited-Time Offers: Creating a sense of urgency can encourage quick decision-making. Offering a limited-time promotion, discount, or bonus can motivate prospects to act before the opportunity passes. Clearly articulate the benefits of acting fast to enhance their motivation.

d. Be Prepared to Handle Objections: Anticipate and prepare for common objections prospects may have. Address concerns clearly and confidently, backing them with data or testimonials. Being well-informed shows you value their concerns and positions you as a credible partner.

e. Follow Up Professionally After Proposals: After sending proposals or quotations, follow up professionally. Reiterate excitement about the potential partnership and invite questions. This keeps communication channels open and allows you to address any lingering doubts they may have.

Closing effectively requires practice and adaptability. Understanding the nuances of each prospect and applying the right techniques will increase your chances of converting leads into loyal customers.

Conclusion

Navigating the sales landscape as a new business can be daunting, but with a strategic approach, it can also be incredibly rewarding. By developing a sound sales strategy, building meaningful relationships, creating a structured sales funnel, leveraging CRM tools, and mastering closing techniques, you position your startup for growth and success. Implement these techniques, adapt to your audience's needs, and watch as your sales efforts translate into meaningful revenue and lasting relationships.

CHAPTER TEN

Navigating Legal and Regulatory Requirements

Navigating Legal and Regulatory Requirements

Starting a business entails navigating a complex landscape of legal and regulatory requirements. Understanding these requirements is crucial for protecting your business and ensuring compliance with laws. This section provides a detailed overview of five key topics: choosing your business structure, registering your business, understanding intellectual property, complying with regulations, and drafting contracts.

1. Choosing Your Business Structure (LLC, Corporation, etc.)

One of the first and most important decisions you will make as a startup founder is choosing the appropriate legal structure for your business. This choice affects various aspects, including liability, tax obligations, and operational complexity.

a. Types of Business Structures

- **Sole Proprietorship:** This is the simplest form of business entity, where the business is owned and operated by a single individual. It requires minimal paperwork and has no formal registration process. However, the owner is personally liable for all business debts and obligations, which can put personal assets at risk.

- **Partnership:** A partnership involves two or more individuals sharing ownership and responsibilities. There are general partnerships, where all partners share liability, and limited partnerships, where some partners have limited liability. Like sole proprietorships, partnerships do not provide liability protection for personal assets.

- **Limited Liability Company (LLC):** An LLC offers the liability protection of a corporation while allowing for flexible tax treatment. Owners (called members) are not personally liable for business debts, protecting personal assets from business liabilities. Additionally, an LLC can choose to be taxed as a sole proprietorship, partnership, or corporation.

- **Corporation:** Corporations are more complex structures that provide limited liability protection. They can issue shares and have a more formal governance structure with a board of directors. There are several types of corporations, including C corporations and S corporations, each with different tax implications. Corporations are subject to more regulations and require ongoing compliance, such as holding annual meetings and maintaining corporate minutes.

b. Factors to Consider When Choosing a Structure

- **Liability:** Assess your tolerance for risk. If your business has a higher risk of lawsuits or debt, an LLC or corporation might be preferable for liability protection.
- **Taxation:** Different structures have varied tax implications. For example, partnerships and sole proprietorships are typically subject to pass-through taxation, while corporations may face double taxation.
- **Cost and Complexity:** Consider the cost of formation and ongoing compliance. Corporations generally incur higher costs and must follow strict regulatory requirements.
- **Investment Needs:** If you plan to seek outside investment, a corporation may be more attractive to investors due to its ability to issue shares.

In summary, selecting the appropriate business structure is critical for your startup and should be made after careful consideration of your business goals, risk tolerance, and financial situation.

2. Registering Your Business and Securing Necessary Licenses

Once you've chosen a business structure, the next step is to register your business and obtain any required licenses or permits. This process varies by location, industry, and legal structure.

a. Business Name Registration

Before you can officially operate, you need to choose and register your business name. Depending on your structure, you may need to register a fictitious name (also known as a "Doing Business As" name or DBA) if your business operates under a name different from your legal name.

- **Checking Name Availability:** Conduct a search in your state's business registry to ensure your desired name is not already in use. Reserving your name can also protect it while you complete the registration process.
- **Trademark Considerations:** If you plan to grow your brand nationally or internationally, consider trademarking your business name and logo to protect your intellectual property.

b. Registering Your Business

Once your name is established, you must register your business with the appropriate state agency.

- **LLC and Corporation Registration:** For LLCs and corporations, you'll need to file Articles of Organization (for LLCs) or Articles of Incorporation (for corporations) with your state's Secretary of State office. This usually involves a filing fee and may require you to provide details about your business, such as its address, name, and management structure.
- **Sole Proprietorships and Partnerships:** Typically, these structures do not require formal registration. However, you may need to register your DBA if applicable.

c. Securing Necessary Licenses and Permits

Depending on your industry and location, you may need various licenses and permits to operate legally. Common types include:

- **Business Licenses:** Most local governments require general business licenses to operate.
- **Industry-Specific Licenses:** Certain industries, such as food service, childcare, healthcare, or finance, often require additional licenses or permits.
- **Zoning Permits:** If you plan to operate a physical location, check local zoning laws to ensure your business type is permitted in your chosen area.
- **Health and Safety Permits:** Businesses that involve health or safety standards may need inspections and certifications.

In conclusion, registering your business and obtaining the necessary licenses is essential to start your operations legally. Failure to comply can result in fines, penalties, or even business closure.

3. Understanding Intellectual Property and Patents

Intellectual property (IP) comprises the creations of the mind, such as inventions, literary and artistic works, designs, symbols, names, and images used in commerce. Protecting your IP is essential for maintaining a competitive edge.

a. Types of Intellectual Property

- **Patents:** A patent grants the inventor exclusive rights to use, manufacture, or sell an invention for a fixed period, usually 20 years. There are different types of patents:

  - **Utility Patents:** For new inventions or functional improvements.
  - **Design Patents:** For new, original, and ornamental designs.
  - **Plant Patents:** For new varieties of plants.

- **Trademarks:** A trademark protects symbols, names, and slogans used to identify goods or services. Unlike patents, trademarks can last indefinitely as long as they are used and renewed periodically.
- **Copyrights:** Copyright protects original works of authorship, such as literature, music, and art. Copyright arises automatically when a work is created and lasts for the life of the author plus 70 years.
- **Trade Secrets:** Trade secrets refer to confidential business information that provides a competitive edge, such as recipes, methods, or formulas. There is no formal registration for trade secrets; protection involves taking steps to keep the information secret.

b. Protecting Your Intellectual Property

- **Conducting IP Audits:** Regularly review your business processes and product offerings to identify potential IP that needs protection.
- **Filing for Protection:** Depending on your needs, file for patents, trademarks, or copyrights with the US Patent and Trademark Office (USPTO) or the Copyright Office.
- **Non-Disclosure Agreements (NDAs):** When sharing sensitive information with partners or employees, use NDAs to protect your trade

secrets.

c. Enforcing Your Rights

Protecting your IP also means enforcing your rights against infringement. This can involve:

- **Monitoring the Market:** Keep an eye on competitors to identify potential IP violations.
- **Legal Action:** If someone infringes upon your IP, you may need to send cease-and-desist letters or pursue legal action.

Understanding and protecting your intellectual property is crucial for maintaining your competitive position and ensuring the success of your startup.

4. Complying with Regulatory Requirements

Every industry has regulatory requirements that businesses must comply with to operate legally. Understanding these regulations is essential to avoid legal pitfalls.

a. Industry Regulations

- **Sector-Specific Regulations:** Depending on your industry, you may be subject to laws and regulations that govern operations. For example, healthcare providers must comply with HIPAA, while financial services companies must adhere to securities regulations.
- **Environmental Regulations:** Businesses that impact the environment may have to comply with federal and state environmental laws. This includes waste disposal, emissions limitations, and chemical storage regulations.

b. Employment Laws

As an employer, you must comply with labor laws that govern employee rights:

– **Wage and Hour Laws:** Ensure compliance with minimum wage laws, overtime pay, and other wage-related regulations.

– **Workplace Safety:** The Occupational Safety and Health Administration (OSHA) sets safety standards that employers must meet to ensure a safe working environment.

– **Anti-Discrimination Laws:** Title VII of the Civil Rights Act prohibits discrimination based on race, color, religion, sex, or national origin. Familiarize yourself with local, state, and federal employment laws.

c. Tax Compliance

Each business structure has different tax obligations. Ensure that you:

- **Obtain an EIN:** An Employer Identification Number (EIN) is required for tax purposes when hiring employees or forming a partnership or corporation.
- **Understand Tax Obligations:** Comply with federal, state, and local tax requirements, including sales tax, income tax, and payroll tax.

d. Ongoing Compliance

Compliance is an ongoing process. Regularly review and update your policies and procedures to account for any regulatory changes. You may need to conduct compliance audits to assess your adherence to applicable laws and regulations.

Staying informed about regulatory requirements and ensuring compliance helps minimize the risk of legal issues.

5. Drafting Contracts and Agreements

Contracts are essential for establishing clear expectations and obligations between parties. Properly drafted contracts protect your business interests and reduce the likelihood of disputes.

a. Types of Business Contracts

- **Partnership Agreements:** If you are starting a business with one or more partners, a partnership agreement outlines each partner's roles, contributions, profit sharing, and procedures for resolving disputes.
- **Operating Agreements:** For LLCs, an operating agreement specifies management structures, member responsibilities, and procedures for adding or removing members.
- **Employment Contracts:** Employment contracts outline the terms of employment, such as job responsibilities, salary, benefits, and termination procedures.
- **Non-Disclosure Agreements (NDAs):** NDAs protect sensitive information by restricting the sharing of confidential business information.

- **Service Contracts:** If you provide services to clients, a service contract outlines the scope of work, payment terms, timelines, and deliverables.

b. Key Elements of a Contract

When drafting contracts, ensure you include the following key elements:

- **Offer and Acceptance:** Clearly define the terms of the offer and specify how acceptance will occur.
- **Consideration:** Document what each party will give or do in the contract — typically involving payment, services, or products.
- **Mutual Agreement:** Ensure that all parties understand and agree to the terms. Clear language helps prevent misunderstandings.
- **Termination Clause:** Outline the circumstances under which parties can terminate the agreement.
- **Governing Law:** Specify which state's laws will govern the contract to avoid jurisdictional issues.

c. Seeking Legal Assistance

While you can draft contracts yourself, seeking legal assistance ensures that your agreements are enforceable, comprehensive, and compliant with applicable laws. An attorney familiar with your industry can provide invaluable guidance.

d. Contract Enforcement and Dispute Resolution

Clearly outline your process for resolving disputes in your contracts. Common mechanisms include:

- **Mediation:** A neutral third party helps facilitate a resolution.
- **Arbitration:** Parties submit their dispute to an arbitrator for a binding decision.
- **Litigation:** Seek resolution through the court system if other options fail.

Enforcing contracts is essential for protecting your business. Establish clear channels for communication to address issues before they escalate into disputes.

Conclusion

Navigating the legal and regulatory landscape is crucial for startups. Understanding the intricacies of business structure, registration, intellectual property, regulatory compliance, and contract drafting can help you establish a solid foundation for your business. Investing the time and resources to ensure legal compliance will not only protect your startup but also pave the way for long-term success.

CHAPTER ELEVEN

Harnessing Technology for Growth

Harnessing Technology for Growth

In today's digital age, leveraging technology is essential for startups to survive and thrive. This chapter dives deep into five critical topics that underscore the significant role technology plays in scaling your business effectively.

1. Identifying the Right Tools and Software for Your Startup

Selecting the right tools and software is the first step in utilizing technology for your startup's growth. Ideally, the tools you choose should enhance productivity, streamline operations, and align with your business goals. Here's how to navigate this decision-making process:

Assess Your Needs: Start by identifying the core functions of your business that require support. Are you looking for solutions for project management, communication, marketing, finance, or customer relationship management (CRM)? Conducting a thorough needs assessment will give you direction.

Research Tools: Once you understand your needs, research the available solutions tailored to those functions. Look for software that is designed specifically for startups or small businesses as they often have features that fit tight budgets and scale well. Popular categories include:

- **Project Management:** Tools like Trello, Asana, and ClickUp offer task assignment, tracking, and deadline management.
- **Communication:** Slack and Microsoft Teams facilitate internal communication, while Zoom and Google Meet support remote meetings.
- **Financial Management:** QuickBooks and Xero assist with accounting, invoicing, and financial reporting.

- **Marketing Automation:** HubSpot and Mailchimp help you manage email campaigns, social media accounts, and customer engagement.

Evaluate Cost vs. Value: Cost is always a consideration, but value is paramount. Software solutions should not only fit into your budget but also provide a return on investment. Consider the time saved, increased output, and improved quality of work versus the ongoing costs of the software.

User Reviews and Trials: Before making a commitment, look up user reviews and request trials or demos. This gives you firsthand experience and insights into potential issues or advantages of the software.

Integration and Scalability: Evaluate how easily the tools can integrate with your existing systems. Additionally, consider the scalability of the software. As your business grows, will the tools still serve your needs, or will you need to invest in new solutions?

Choosing the right tools and software can significantly streamline operations and free up resources to focus on growth and innovation.

2. Understanding Cloud Computing and Its Benefits

Cloud computing is the delivery of computing services over the internet, allowing for flexible resources, faster innovation, and economies of scale. Understanding cloud computing can equip startups with the ability to operate more efficiently and effectively.

Types of Cloud Services: There are generally three types of cloud services that businesses can leverage:

- **Infrastructure as a Service (IaaS):** Services like Amazon Web Services and Microsoft Azure provide virtualized computing resources over the internet. This allows startups to rent servers and storage without investing in physical hardware.
- **Platform as a Service (PaaS):** Platforms such as Google Cloud Platform and Heroku offer environments for developers to build applications without worrying about maintaining the infrastructure. This speeds up development processes and allows startups to focus on coding and design.
- **Software as a Service (SaaS):** Tools like Google Workspace and Salesforce are delivered via the cloud and are accessible from anywhere, which is suitable for remote work and collaboration.

Cost Efficiency: Cloud computing reduces capital expenditure on hardware and software. Pay-as-you-go pricing models mean startups only pay for what they use, allowing for budget flexibility that traditional IT setups often do not provide.

Scalability: Startups can scale their operations efficiently through cloud services. As your business grows, cloud resources can be adjusted according to demand, without the need for significant investment in new hardware.

Collaboration: Cloud computing facilitates collaboration among team members, regardless of location. With cloud-based tools, files can be accessed, shared, and edited in real-time, enhancing teamwork and productivity.

Security and Backup: Renowned cloud service providers usually incorporate robust security measures, including data encryption and multi-factor authentication. Furthermore, automatic backups ensure that critical data is protected against loss.

Familiarizing yourself with cloud computing will position your startup to leverage its full range of benefits, enabling flexibility and enhanced operational capabilities.

3. Integrating AI and Automation into Your Business Processes

Artificial Intelligence (AI) and automation technologies can revolutionize how startups operate, driving efficiencies and enabling smarter decision-making.

Identifying Tasks for Automation: Start by analyzing repetitive tasks that consume valuable resources. Common areas often ripe for automation include:

- **Customer Service:** AI-powered chatbots can handle queries, provide instant replies, and assist customers 24/7, freeing up human staff for more complex tasks.
- **Marketing Automation:** Tools like HubSpot and Mailchimp allow you to automate email campaigns, follow-ups, and social media posts, ensuring your marketing efforts are consistent and timely.
- **Sales Processes:** CRM systems integrate AI for lead scoring, automating outreach, and optimizing sales strategies based on customer behavior.

Selecting AI Tools: Choose AI tools that align with your specific needs. Evaluate products that utilize machine learning to gain insights on customer preferences and trends. Look for user-friendly interfaces that do not require extensive technical skills.

Data Collection and Usage: Successful AI implementations are heavily reliant on data. Collect relevant data points from various customer interactions to train your AI systems accurately. For instance, collecting feedback from customer service interactions will help refine chatbot responses.

Monitor and Optimize: After implementing AI and automation tools, continuously monitor their performance. Analyze metrics to determine effectiveness and make adjustments as required. This iterative optimization will lead to greater efficiencies and improved output.

Integrating AI and automation not only enhances the efficiency of your operations but also allows you to dedicate more time to strategic growth initiatives.

4. Cybersecurity: Protecting Your Startup Data

As startups increasingly rely on technology, cybersecurity must be a priority. Protecting sensitive data and maintaining customer trust is vital for long-term success.

Understanding Cyber Threats: Startups face several cyber threats, including ransomware, phishing attacks, and data breaches. Understanding these threats will help you develop strategies to mitigate risks.

Conduct a Risk Assessment: Begin by conducting a cybersecurity risk assessment to identify vulnerabilities within your systems. This includes evaluating both software applications and employee practices.

Implement Strong Security Protocols:

- **Employee Training:** Train employees on safe digital practices, including recognizing phishing attempts and securely handling sensitive data.
- **Access Control:** Use role-based access controls to limit access to sensitive information based on necessity. This safeguards against internal threats.
- **Regular Software Updates:** Keep your software and systems updated to protect against vulnerabilities.

Utilizing Cybersecurity Tools: Invest in cybersecurity solutions like firewalls, anti-virus software, and intrusion detection systems. Services such as VPNs (Virtual Private Networks) for remote work can add an additional layer of security.

Develop an Incident Response Plan: In the event of a security breach or attack, having a robust incident response plan in place can minimize damage. Outline the steps your team should follow to contain the attack, assess the damage, and communicate with stakeholders.

Cybersecurity is not just about protection; it is about ensuring trust and reliability in your startup's operations.

5. Utilizing Data Analytics for Informed Decision Making

Data analytics involves analyzing data sets to identify patterns and insights that inform decision-making. By leveraging analytics, startups can derive actionable insights to enhance performance and strategically grow.

Types of Data Analytics:

- **Descriptive Analytics:** This type analyzes historical data to understand past performance. Metrics like sales figures, web traffic, and customer feedback can reveal trends and performance insights.
- **Predictive Analytics:** By employing statistical algorithms and machine learning techniques, predictive analytics forecasts future outcomes based on historical data. If your startup notices trends in customer spending, for instance, you can apply predictive analytics to anticipate future sales.
- **Prescriptive Analytics:** This goes beyond prediction by recommending actions based on data analysis. It uses algorithms to advise on the best course of action, like pricing strategies or inventory levels.

Choosing the Right Analytics Tools:
Select analytics software that aligns with your goals. Platforms like Google Analytics, Tableau, and Microsoft Power BI offer various features for data collection, analysis, and visualization.

Data Collection Strategies: Collect data from multiple sources, including customer interactions, social media analytics, and website performance metrics. The more comprehensive your data collection, the more accurate your insights will be.

Creating a Data-Driven Culture: Encourage a data-driven culture within your organization. Train employees to view data as a valuable resource for decision-making rather than relying solely on intuition.

Iterating Based on Insights: Use insights gathered from data analytics to iterate on your products, marketing strategies, and customer engagement practices. Continuously monitor the effects of changes based on data feedback to refine your operations further.

Harnessing data analytics will enable your startup to make informed decisions that are grounded in reality, enhancing your competitive edge and fostering sustainable growth.

Conclusion

In summary, adopting a technological framework for growth is imperative in a highly competitive landscape. By carefully selecting essential tools, embracing the cloud, leveraging AI and automation, securing your data, and using analytics for decision-making, startups can significantly enhance their operational capabilities and drive strategic growth. The integration of these elements into your startup's blueprint lays the foundation for sustained success and innovation.

CHAPTER TWELVE

Scaling Your Startup

Scaling Your Startup

Scaling a startup is one of the most exciting and pivotal phases in the entrepreneurial journey. It represents the transition from a fledgling company seeking stability to a thriving business poised for growth and expansion. This chapter delves into five critical topics that will guide you through the scaling process, including when to scale, strategies for expanding offerings, entering new markets, building partnerships, and monitoring key performance indicators (KPIs).

1. Assessing When to Scale Your Business

Scaling is a significant step that requires careful consideration and planning. Before diving into this phase, it is essential to assess whether your startup is ready.

Signs Your Business Is Ready to Scale:

- **Strong Demand:** If you notice consistent demand for your product or service, it can be a strong indicator that you are ready to scale. This information can be gathered from customer feedback, sales data, or market research.
- **Stable Revenue Stream:** A steady and growing revenue stream is crucial before scaling operations. Ensure that your monthly earnings show consistent growth over several months, indicating that your business model is sound.
- **Efficient Processes:** Your internal processes must be running smoothly. Analyze your operations, production, and distribution systems. If these are scalable—meaning they can handle an increase in demand without significant overhauls—you're better positioned to grow.
- **Positive Customer Feedback:** If your customers rave about your product and you observe low churn rates, this indicates that you offer value,

making it an opportune time to expand your reach.

- **Financial Health:** Before scaling, having a solid financial foundation is essential. Review your cash flow, profit margins, and overall financial health. Ensure you have the capital (internal or external) to support scaling efforts.

Key Considerations for Scaling:

- **Market Research:** Conduct thorough market research to confirm there is ample room for growth in your current market or new markets you're considering.
- **Competitive Landscape:** Analyze the competitive landscape to understand if your business can stand out and what barriers to entry exist.
- **Scalability of Business Model:** Evaluate whether your business model is designed for growth. For example, a subscription-based model typically offers better scalability compared to a service-based model requiring more human resources.

By carefully assessing these factors, you can determine the right time to embark on your scaling journey, setting the foundation for future success.

2. Strategies for Expanding Your Product Line or Services

Once you've assessed that your business is ready to scale, the next step may involve expanding your product line or service offerings.

Strategies for Successful Expansion:

- **Customer-Centric Approach:** Begin by evaluating your existing customers' needs and preferences. Gather feedback through surveys, interviews, or customer reviews to understand what additional features or products they may desire. For instance, if your startup sells fitness equipment, consider expanding into fitness apparel or accessories based on customer requests.
- **Market Trends:** Stay informed about industry trends and shifts in consumer demand. Utilize tools like Google Trends, social media analytics, and competitor analysis to identify gaps in the market that your startup can fill.
- **Complementary Products:** Consider offering complementary products that align with your existing offerings. For instance, a company

specializing in coffee could expand by offering coffee accessories like grinders, mugs, or subscriptions for specialty coffee.

- **Pilot Programs:** Before fully launching new products or services, consider pilot programs or limited releases to gauge interest and collect valuable customer feedback.
- **Strategic Partnerships:** Collaborate with other businesses in related fields to co-develop or cross-promote new products or services. This strategy can alleviate some risk associated with new offerings.

Implementation and Testing:

- **Market Testing:** Launch the expansion in a controlled environment or a limited geographic area to test receptiveness. Analyze sales data, customer feedback, and the overall success of the launch to inform full-scale rollouts.
- **Iterative Development:** Employ an iterative approach to refine your offerings continuously based on customer feedback. Be responsive to suggestions and willing to adapt to ensure your expanded product line resonates with your audience.

Expanding your product line or service offerings can significantly impact your startup's growth trajectory. By carefully researching your customers' needs and assessing market trends, you can make informed decisions that bolster your scaling efforts.

3. Entering New Markets: Challenges and Opportunities

One of the most effective ways to scale your startup is to enter new markets—whether geographically, demographically, or through new business channels.

Assessing New Markets:

- **Market Research:** Conduct comprehensive research on potential new markets. Analyze demographics, consumer behavior, existing competition, and market demand. Utilize surveys, focus groups, and data analysis to gather insights.
- **Regulatory Environment:** Understand the legal and regulatory landscape of the new market. This includes trade laws, taxation, labor laws, and any licensing requirements that may impact your expansion.

- **Cultural Considerations:** Cultural nuances can significantly affect how your product or service is received. Conducting cultural assessments or employing local experts can provide insights into how to tailor your marketing and customer communication strategies.

Challenges of Market Entry:

- **Cultural Barriers:** These can impact perception and acceptance of your brand. Successful entry often requires localized marketing strategies and understanding regional preferences.
- **Competition:** New markets may have existing competitors with established customer loyalty. It's essential to identify these competitors and determine how your brand can differentiate itself through unique value propositions.
- **Operational Costs:** Entering a new market often comes with new operational expenses, such as hiring local staff or establishing a distribution network. These costs can add pressure to your cash flow, especially during the initial stages.

Strategies for Successful Market Entry:

- **Pilot Strategy:** Similar to product line expansion, start with a pilot program in a new market. This minimizes risk and allows for gathering insights before committing significant resources.
- **Partnerships and Alliances:** Collaborate with local businesses or influencers to gain credibility and insights into the market.
- **Gradual Expansion:** Plan a phased approach to expanding. Launch your product in a small area of the new market first, then gradually widen your reach based on initial results.

Opportunities:

- **Increased Customer Base:** Expanding to new markets opens access to a larger customer base, potentially increasing sales and brand loyalty.
- **Diversification:** Reducing reliance on a single market can stabilize your business during fluctuations.

By strategically assessing new markets and implementing a well-planned entry strategy, startups can tap into substantial growth potential, navigating challenges while seizing opportunities.

4. Building Partnerships to Drive Growth

Building partnerships can significantly enhance your startup's ability to scale. Collaborating with others allows startups to leverage shared resources, networks, and expertise.

Types of Partnerships:

- **Strategic Alliances:** These are collaborations between businesses that are mutually beneficial. They usually involve sharing technology, knowledge, or expertise.
- **Joint Ventures:** In this scenario, two or more businesses create a new entity, sharing both risks and rewards. Joint ventures can be an effective way to enter a new market with a local partner who knows the terrain.
- **Affiliate Partnerships:** Promoting each other's products or services can yield mutual benefits. This is particularly effective in the digital space, where affiliates can earn commissions on sales they generate.

Benefits of Partnerships:

- **Resource Sharing:** Partnerships can reduce operational costs through shared marketing, technology, or innovations.
- **Broadened Reach:** Collaborating with another business or influencer provides access to their customer base, enhancing brand visibility and awareness.
- **Knowledge and Expertise:** Leveraging partners with different skills or experiences can bolster your startup's competencies, leading to improved product offerings or efficient processes.

Building Successful Partnerships:

- **Identify Potential Partners:** Look for companies that complement your offerings and share similar values and goals. Networking, industry events, and platforms like LinkedIn can help in identifying individuals or organizations that align with your objectives.
- **Establish Clear Goals:** Be transparent about what you aim to achieve through the partnership. Establishing mutually beneficial goals will

create a solid foundation for collaboration.

- **Regular Communication:** Maintaining open lines of communication is vital for building and sustaining partnerships. Schedule regular check-ins to discuss progress and address any challenges.
- **Legal Considerations:** Draft clear agreements outlining roles, responsibilities, and performance expectations. Legal agreements should account for profit-sharing, intellectual property rights, and exit strategies.

Case Example:

Consider a small clothing brand that partners with a local influencer. The brand benefits from the influencer's established audience, while the influencer gains access to exclusive promotional items, enhancing their content. This partnership can drive traffic to both parties and foster growth.

By strategically building and nurturing partnerships, your startup can align with others to accelerate growth and capitalize on shared opportunities.

5. Monitoring Key Performance Indicators (KPIs)

Monitoring KPIs is essential in tracking progress during the scaling phase. Effective use of KPIs helps measure success, informs decision-making, and facilitates adjustments to strategy as necessary.

Identifying Relevant KPIs:

- **Revenue Growth Rate:** This is a critical KPI that indicates how quickly your startup is growing in terms of revenue. A healthy growth rate will signal the overall health and sustainability of your business.
- **Customer Acquisition Cost (CAC):** Understanding how much it costs to acquire a new customer is essential for evaluating marketing efficiency. Reducing CAC through strategies such as targeted ads will improve profitability.
- **Customer Lifetime Value (CLV):** Knowing the total value a customer brings to your business provides insight into how much you can spend on customer acquisition while still being profitable.
- **Churn Rate:** Monitoring the percentage of customers who stop using your service or product is vital, especially for subscription-based models. A high churn rate indicates potential issues with customer satisfaction or product-market fit.

- **Gross Margin:** Gross margin indicates the difference between revenue and the cost of goods sold, expressed as a percentage of revenue. A healthy gross margin is a good indication of a scalable business model.

Using KPIs Effectively:

- **Set Clear Performance Targets:** Establish specific, measurable targets for each KPI. For example, if your CLV is currently $100, set a target to increase it to $120 over the next quarter.
- **Dashboards and Reporting Tools:** Utilize dashboard software to visually track KPIs over time. Tools like Google Analytics, Tableau, or custom reporting dashboards can provide real-time insights into business performance.
- **Regular Reviews:** Schedule regular review meetings to analyze performance data. Using these insights, adjust strategies or operations to align with your scaling goals.
- **Itcratc Bascd on Data:** Usc KPI data to inform your stratcgic decisions. If you notice declining gross margins, investigate the causes and re-evaluate pricing or cost-management strategies.

Monitoring KPIs is an ongoing process vital to ensuring your startup is on track for sustainable growth during the scaling phase. By focusing on key metrics and being responsive to insights, you'll position your startup for long-term success.

Conclusion

Scaling a startup is an exhilarating yet challenging journey. By assessing when to scale, expanding your product line thoughtfully, exploring new markets, leveraging partnerships, and closely monitoring KPIs, you can navigate this pivotal phase successfully. Each step taken in this process is an exciting opportunity to enhance your startup's impact and sustainability, ultimately leading you to achieve your broader vision as an entrepreneur.

CHAPTER THIRTEEN

Navigating Challenges and Setbacks

Navigating Challenges and Setbacks

Navigating the world of startups can be a thrilling journey filled with innovation and creativity, but it can also be a tumultuous ride fraught with unforeseen challenges and setbacks. This chapter will explore common startup challenges, strategies for managing stress and maintaining resilience, the importance of pivoting when necessary, insights gained from case studies of successful startup failures, and the value of building a strong support network.

1. Identifying Common Startup Challenges

Understanding Startup Challenges

Every startup faces its unique set of challenges, but many fall under certain common categories. Understanding these challenges is critical for any entrepreneur aiming to prepare for and mitigate them effectively.

1.1. Funding Shortages

One of the most significant challenges startups face is accessing sufficient funding. High initial costs, personal investment, and securing investor confidence are common hurdles. Startups often struggle with cash flow issues, affecting their ability to operate smoothly, pay employees, and invest in growth.

1.2. Market Competition

In a rapidly evolving business landscape, competition can be fierce. Many startups enter saturated markets, which can make it difficult to carve out a niche. Entrepreneurs must constantly innovate and differentiate their product or service to stay relevant and competitive.

1.3. Operational Complexities

Startups commonly face operational difficulties, including supply chain management, hiring the right talent, and creating efficient processes. Many founders lack the experience or resources to establish smooth operations, leading to mismanagement and inefficiencies.

1.4. Customer Acquisition

Establishing a customer base is crucial for startup success, yet it can be challenging. Startups often struggle with marketing strategies, identifying their target audience, and generating leads. High customer acquisition costs can severely limit growth potential.

1.5. Regulatory Hurdles

Navigating legal and regulatory requirements can be a daunting task for startups. Compliance with local, state, and federal laws is essential but complicated. Ignoring regulations or failing to comply can result in costly penalties and may even jeopardize the business.

2. Strategies for Managing Stress and Maintaining Resilience

The Importance of Mental Health for Entrepreneurs

Managing stress and maintaining resilience is vital for startup founders. The emotional toll of overcoming challenges can lead to burnout and poor decision-making, which can ultimately harm the business.

2.1. Time Management Practices

Effective time management can help alleviate stress. Founders should prioritize tasks by urgency and importance. Techniques such as the Pomodoro Technique—where work periods are broken up with short breaks—can enhance focus and productivity.

2.2. Setting Realistic Goals

Entrepreneurs can mitigate stress by setting achievable goals. Breaking down larger objectives into smaller, manageable milestones can lead to a sense of accomplishment and motivation. This approach helps prevent overwhelming feelings that can result from trying to achieve too much at once.

2.3. Mindfulness and Relaxation Techniques

Practicing mindfulness can aid founders in managing stress. Techniques such as meditation, yoga, or even deep-breathing exercises can reduce anxiety levels. Regularly taking time to engage in hobbies or physical activities can also help clear the mind and recharge emotional batteries.

2.4. Seeking Professional Help

When stress becomes overwhelming, seeking help from mental health professionals can be incredibly beneficial. Therapists or coaches can provide valuable coping strategies and emotional support, empowering entrepreneurs to navigate their emotional landscapes more effectively.

2.5. Building a Supportive Company Culture

Establishing a positive workplace culture helps sustain resilience among teams. Encouraging open communication, providing opportunities for team bonding, and recognizing accomplishments can foster a supportive environment that enables everyone to pull together during challenging times.

3. Pivoting: When and How to Change Course

Understanding the Importance of Pivoting

Pivoting refers to the strategic decision to change direction based on lessons learned or external factors. While it may seem daunting, pivoting can be a critical element in achieving long-term success.

3.1. Recognizing the Need to Pivot

The first step in recognizing the need to pivot is collecting and analyzing data. If user feedback or market research indicates that the original idea is not resonating with customers, it might be time to explore alternative approaches. Indicators such as declining sales, negative customer feedback, or shifts in market demand should prompt leaders to consider change.

3.2. Types of Pivots

Startups can pivot in various ways, including:

- **Product Pivot**: Altering or reimagining the product to better meet customer needs.
- **Customer Segment Pivot**: Focusing on a different target audience that may respond more favorably to the product or service.
- **Business Model Pivot**: Changing the way the business generates revenue, such as from a product-based model to a subscription model.

3.3. Creating a Pivot Plan

Once the decision to pivot has been made, creating a structured pivot plan is essential. This should outline the new direction, objectives, timelines, and necessary resources. Key stakeholders should be informed of the changes, and everyone on the team ought to understand the rationale behind the pivot.

3.4. Testing the New Direction

Before fully committing to a pivot, conducting small-scale tests can help mitigate risks. Gathering feedback on prototypes, pilot programs, or marketing strategies enables startups to refine their approach based on real-world data.

3.5. Maintaining Team Morale During a Pivot

Change can be unsettling for teams, so keeping morale high is crucial. Communicate openly about the reasons behind the pivot and its potential benefits. Involving team members in the decision-making process can also empower them and foster a sense of ownership over the new direction.

4. Learning from Failure: Case Studies of Successful Startups

Embracing Failure as an Opportunity for Growth

Failure is often viewed negatively; however, some of the most successful startups have risen from the ashes of failure. Analyzing case studies can provide valuable insights into resilience and adaptation.

4.1. Airbnb: Overcoming Initial Struggles

Airbnb founders Brian Chesky and Joe Gebbia originally struggled to gain traction with their home-sharing idea. Early ventures were met with skepticism, and they nearly ran out of money. However, they learned from user feedback and adapted their marketing strategy, focusing on high-quality photography of listings. Today, Airbnb is a household name.

4.2. Pinterest: Evolving from a Different Vision

Pinterest began as a mobile app called "Twant" designed to help users share shopping lists. Initial attempts didn't resonate with users, leading founders to revisit their vision. They pivoted to create a visual bookmarking tool based on user interests. This shift paved the way for its current success as a leading platform for discovery and inspiration.

4.3. Slack: Responding to User Needs

Before it became a dominant communication platform, Slack began as an internal tool for a gaming company called Tiny Speck. After the game failed to gain popularity, the founders pivoted to focus on refining this communication tool and launched it as a standalone product. Today, Slack is widely used in various industries.

4.4. Twitter: From Obscure Podcasting Platform

Twitter originated from a podcasting platform called Odeo. However, when Apple announced the launch of its podcasting platform, the founders had to pivot quickly. They shifted their focus to microblogging, creating a real-time communication tool that facilitated connections. This adaptation transformed Twitter into a social media powerhouse.

4.5. Instagram: Learning and Growing through Acquisitions

Instagram started as a check-in app called Burbn but struggled to differentiate itself amidst numerous competitors. The founders realized users favored photo-sharing features, prompting a pivot to focus exclusively on that aspect. The platform quickly gained popularity and was eventually acquired by Facebook for $1 billion in 2012.

5. Building a Support Network: Mentorship and Advisory Boards

The Importance of Community in Overcoming Challenges

Building a robust support network is crucial for navigating the ups and downs of entrepreneurship. Mentorship and advisory boards can provide invaluable guidance, insight, and encouragement.

5.1. Seeking Out Mentors

Mentorship can take various forms, from formal programs to informal relationships. Successful entrepreneurs can offer advice, share experiences, and provide valuable networking connections. Founders should actively seek out mentors who align with their industry or can provide complementary skills.

5.2. Forming an Advisory Board

An advisory board consists of experienced industry professionals who offer strategic guidance to startups. Unlike a board of directors, advisory boards do not have formal governance responsibilities. By leveraging the expertise of advisory board members, startups can make more informed decisions and navigate challenges effectively.

5.3. Networking Opportunities

Attending industry conferences, networking events, and workshops allows entrepreneurs to connect with peers and industry leaders. Establishing relationships within a professional network can lead to not only mentorship opportunities but also partnerships and collaborations.

5.4. Leveraging Online Communities

Online platforms such as LinkedIn, Facebook groups, or industry-specific forums offer avenues for entrepreneurs to engage with their peers. Participating in discussions, seeking advice, and sharing resources within these communities can provide significant support and insights.

5.5. Building Emotional Support Systems

Beyond professional networks, emotional support systems are also critical for entrepreneurs. Friends, family, and fellow entrepreneurs can provide encouragement, empathy, and a sounding board for ideas. Building a well-rounded support system leads to improved mental health and resilience.

Conclusion

Navigating challenges and setbacks is an inevitable part of the entrepreneurial journey. By identifying common challenges, managing stress, pivoting when necessary, learning from failures, and leveraging support networks, entrepreneurs can build resilience and enhance their chances of success. Embracing these elements creates a foundation for sustained growth and innovation, allowing visionaries to transform their dreams into thriving businesses.

The road to success is rarely linear; understanding and preparing for challenges can empower entrepreneurs to navigate the complexities of the startup landscape with confidence and purpose.

CHAPTER FOURTEEN

Engaging and Retaining Customers

Engaging and Retaining Customers

The success of any startup relies not only on acquiring customers but also on retaining them. Customer engagement and retention are critical components that can significantly impact profits, brand loyalty, and competitive advantage. This chapter will delve into five key themes: understanding customer acquisition vs. retention, creating exceptional customer experiences, developing loyalty programs and incentives, gathering customer feedback to improve offerings, and the role of customer service in startups.

1. Understanding Customer Acquisition vs. Retention

Customer Acquisition Customer acquisition refers to the process of gaining new customers for your business. It involves marketing strategies, sales tactics, and outreach efforts impacted by market conditions and competition. Acquiring customers is essential, especially for startups, to build a customer base and generate revenue. Typically, this process comprises several stages:

- **Awareness:** Potential customers become aware of your product or service through marketing campaigns, referrals, social media, or search engines.
- **Consideration:** At this stage, customers evaluate your offerings against competitors and seek information that builds trust—such as customer testimonials or case studies.
- **Conversion:** This is the final step where a potential customer makes a purchase decision. Effective sales strategies can significantly enhance conversion rates.

Customer Retention On the other hand, customer retention refers to the strategies and actions businesses undertake to keep existing customers coming back for more. Retained customers are often more valuable than newly acquired ones because they generate repeat business. Advantages of high customer retention rates include:

- **Cost Savings**: It's typically less expensive to maintain existing customers than to attract new ones. The costs associated with acquiring new customers include advertising, promotions, and sales efforts.
- **Increased Lifetime Value (LTV)**: Loyal customers tend to spend more over their lifetime compared to new customers, thus enhancing overall profitability.
- **Word-of-Mouth Marketing**: Satisfied customers are likely to share their positive experiences with others, providing free marketing for your brand.

In summary, while customer acquisition is vital for growth, focusing solely on it can lead to problems. Without adequate attention on retention, a startup may find itself in a cycle of constantly needing to acquire new customers, driven partly by neglect of its existing customer base. An ideal strategy should prioritize both acquisition and retention, considering their intertwined nature.

2. Creating Exceptional Customer Experiences

The customer experience (CX) is defined by how customers perceive their interactions with your startup across all touchpoints. Crafting exceptional CX is critical to engagement and retention. Here are some strategies to enhance your customer experience:

- **Personalization**: Tailoring experiences, offers, and communications to fit individual customer preferences can significantly enhance satisfaction. Techniques include using customer data to create personalized marketing messages or recommending products based on previous purchases.
- **Consistency Across Channels**: Customers interact with your brand through various channels, including social media, websites, and physical stores. Ensuring a consistent experience across all channels fosters trust and reliability. Consistency in branding, messaging, and customer service sets clear expectations.

- **User-Friendly Interfaces**: Whether it's your website, app, or physical location, a user-friendly interface is essential. Consider implementing website optimizations, responsive designs, and streamlined checkout processes to improve ease of use and attract customers.
- **Proactive Support**: Anticipate customer needs and provide support before they reach out. For instance, offering live chat on your website or sending proactive updates about order status can create a seamless experience.
- **Emotional Connection**: Connecting with customers on an emotional level can enhance loyalty. Brands that craft storytelling and create narratives around their products resonate better with customers. Consider how your service or product solves pain points and enhances customers' lives.

A positive customer experience is paramount for creating loyal customers. Businesses that prioritize CX see improved customer satisfaction and long-term engagement.

3. Developing Loyalty Programs and Incentives

Loyalty programs are structured marketing strategies designed to encourage customers to continue buying from your brand. Effective loyalty programs create emotional engagement and provide tangible rewards. Here are key components to consider:

- **Points-Based Systems**: This is a common structure where customers earn points for every purchase, which they can redeem for rewards or discounts. For example, a coffee shop may offer 10 points per purchase, with 100 points redeemable for a free drink.
- **Tiered Rewards**: Implementing a tier system encourages customers to spend more to reach higher levels for better rewards. For instance, customers at a silver tier receive 5% off, while gold members enjoy 15% off, enticing customers to increase their engagement.
- **Referral Incentives**: Encourage existing customers to refer new customers by providing rewards or discounts. This not only fosters customer loyalty but also builds your customer base through word-of-mouth.
- **Exclusive Offers**: Create a sense of exclusivity by offering special promotions, events, or products to loyalty program members. This could entail early access to new products or members-only discounts.

- **Feedback-Based Rewards**: Engaging customers in the development of your products and services through surveys or input sessions can encourage loyalty. Offering rewards or discounts for participation reconfirm customers' value.

Loyalty programs should not feel transactional. Instead, they should build a sense of belonging and community around your brand, thereby incentivizing customers to remain engaged and committed.

4. Gathering Customer Feedback to Improve Offerings

Customer feedback is an invaluable resource that can help shape and improve your offerings. Effective feedback mechanisms and strategies include:

- **Surveys and Questionnaires**: After customer interactions, gather feedback through surveys to gauge satisfaction levels. Platforms like SurveyMonkey or Typeform can make this process easy. Consider open-ended questions to gather qualitative insights alongside quantitative scores.
- **Social Media and Online Reviews**: Monitor social media channels and sites like Trustpilot or Yelp. Engaging with customers who leave reviews—both favorable and unfavorable—demonstrates that you value their opinions and are committed to improvement.
- **Customer Focus Groups**: Conduct focus groups with select customers to gather in-depth feedback about specific products or services. This direct conversation allows companies to grasp customers' experiences and pain points deeper.
- **Usability Testing**: For technological products, conduct usability testing by observing how customers interact with your product or service. This can expose areas of friction and opportunities for refinement.
- **Net Promoter Score (NPS)**: Tracking your NPS provides insights into customer loyalty by measuring how willing customers are to recommend your product. A high NPS indicates satisfied customers, while a low score signals the need for urgent changes.

Using feedback to make changes not only improves your product or service but also demonstrates to customers that their voices matter. This builds trust and fosters loyalty.

5. The Role of Customer Service in Startups

Customer service is the frontline of customer retention. Exceptional service can differentiate your startup in a crowded marketplace. Key aspects include:

- **Responsive Communication**: Quick and efficient responses to customer inquiries—via email, social media, phone, or chat—are essential in a world that demands speedy solutions. Ensure that your customer service team is accessible and trained to handle queries effectively.
- **Empathy and Understanding**: Train your support team to listen actively and empathize when customers face issues. Customers who feel valued are more likely to remain loyal.
- **Training and Empowerment**: Ensure your customer service representatives are well trained. Equipping them with the knowledge and authority to make decisions can lead to quicker resolutions and satisfied customers.
- **Multichannel Support**: Customers should have multiple avenues to reach your team—whether through a phone line, chat support, email, or social media. Offering various channels creates convenience and caters to customer preferences.
- **Follow-up**: Don't let interactions end once an issue is resolved. Follow up with customers to ensure they are satisfied with the resolution. A simple email or call can show that you care about their experience, strengthening their loyalty.

In conclusion, customer service is crucial for retaining customers. Startups that prioritize responsive, empathetic, and effective service build strong connections and loyalty with their customer base.

Conclusion

Engaging and retaining customers is vital for the long-term success of any startup. Understanding the nuances between customer acquisition and retention, creating exceptional customer experiences, developing effective loyalty programs, leveraging customer feedback, and providing outstanding customer service are all critical components in building lasting relationships.

Investing in these areas not only enhances customer satisfaction but also drives long-term profitability. By focusing on the entire customer journey and fostering meaningful connections, startups can differentiate themselves in competitive markets and build a loyal customer base that sustains their business for years to come.

This breakdown provides an in-depth exploration of each of the topics outlined in this chapter, emphasizing strategies, tools, and best practices for engaging and retaining customers effectively. If you would like to expand further on any specific section or add more detail, please let me know!

CHAPTER FIFTEEN

The Road to Innovation

The Road to Innovation

1. Fostering a Culture of Continuous Improvement

Understanding Continuous Improvement

Continuous improvement refers to an ongoing effort to enhance products, services, or processes. The philosophy promotes small, incremental changes that collectively lead to significant improvements over time. It's a mindset that urges individuals and teams within an organization to apply critical thinking to their everyday tasks while striving for excellence.

Building the Right Environment

To foster a culture of continuous improvement, an organization must first assess its environment. Key elements required include:

- **Leadership Commitment:** Leaders should model the behaviors they wish to instill. When leadership actively participates in improvement initiatives, it sends a message to all employees that such efforts are valued.
- **Employee Empowerment:** Employees should feel empowered and encouraged to voice ideas and concerns. Providing platforms for them to share insights, whether through suggestion boxes, meetings, or brainstorming sessions, fosters an inclusive improvement culture.

- **Open Communication:** Maintaining open lines of communication within teams helps identify issues early and encourages members to share success stories as well as failures. Transparency builds trust among employees and leadership.

Implementation Strategies

Successful continuous improvement interventions often utilize frameworks like Lean, Six Sigma, or Total Quality Management (TQM). Each framework offers tools and methodologies that promote a systematic approach to identifying waste, reducing defects, and driving efficiency.

- **Training Programs:** Regular training sessions on improvement principles and tools are essential. Employees should be equipped with knowledge about methodologies so they can apply them in their daily tasks.
- **Establish Metrics:** Implement key performance indicators (KPIs) that measure progress. Tracking performance data helps teams understand the impact of their improvements and adjust efforts based on results.
- **Encourage Experimentation:** Foster an atmosphere where experimentation is encouraged. When teams feel free to test new approaches, establish pilot programs, or engage in trial-and-error, they are likely to uncover innovative solutions.

Recognition and Reward

Recognizing employees' efforts in continuous improvement is crucial. Whether through formal recognition programs, monetary incentives, or simple verbal praise, acknowledgment bolsters motivation:

- **Spotlight Innovations:** Regularly highlight teams or individuals who have successfully implemented improvements. Sharing their success stories can inspire others.
- **Reward Programs:** Consider developing reward systems tied to specific improvement outcomes or goals. This could range from bonuses to additional time off or professional development opportunities.

Challenges to Overcome

A culture of continuous improvement may face challenges, such as resistance to change or limited resources. To mitigate these issues, organizations should:

- **Listen to Employee Feedback:** If resistance arises, seek to understand the employees' concerns. Sometimes, fears about change stem from a lack of understanding or insufficient communication.
- **Provide Resources:** Ensure teams have the necessary tools and resources to pursue their improvement efforts. This may include technology, time, personnel support, or access to expertise.

Conclusion

A culture of continuous improvement permeates an organization's ethos, encouraging every team member to contribute to refinement efforts. By nurturing an approach grounded in learning, empowerment, and recognition, organizations can facilitate meaningful transformations that lead to sustainable innovation.

2. Integrating Customer Feedback into Product Development

The Importance of Customer Feedback

Customer feedback is vital in product development as it provides insights directly from the individuals using the product. Understanding customers' needs, pain points, and expectations allows companies to create products that genuinely address market demands.

Collecting Feedback

There are numerous methods to collect customer feedback efficiently:

- **Surveys and Questionnaires:** Distributing surveys via email or website pop-ups is a common method. These can be short and focused on specific aspects of the product/service.
- **Customer Interviews:** Conducting one-on-one interviews yields in-depth insights. They allow for open-ended questions, facilitating deeper exploration into customer thoughts and experiences.
- **Focus Groups:** Gathering a small group of target customers to discuss a product concept or existing product offers qualitative insights. It encourages dynamic discussions and diverse perspectives.
- **Online Reviews and Social Media:** Monitoring reviews on platforms such as Yelp or social media channels can uncover trends in customer sentiment. Customers often share candid opinions publicly.
- **Usability Testing:** Inviting customers to interact with prototypes or beta versions can reveal usability issues. This hands-on feedback is valuable for practical adjustments prior to full-scale launches.

Analyzing Feedback

Collecting feedback is only the first step; companies must then analyze the data for meaningful insights. Techniques include:

- **Categorization:** Organizing feedback into categories (e.g., product features, support issues, pricing) helps in identifying common themes and trends.
- **Quantitative Analysis:** Using metrics such as Net Promoter Score (NPS) or Customer Satisfaction Score (CSAT) helps gauge overall satisfaction levels.
- **Qualitative Analysis:** Delving into open-ended responses can provide rich insights into customer thoughts. Look for recurring phrases or sentiments to identify underlying feelings.

Integration into Product Development

Once feedback is collected and analyzed, it must be integrated into the product development lifecycle:

- **Prioritization:** Not all feedback can be acted upon immediately. Teams should prioritize changes based on their potential impact on customer satisfaction and business goals.
- **Iterative Design:** Embracing an agile methodology allows teams to make incremental adjustments based on feedback. Regularly updating the product based on user responses keeps it relevant and user-centric.
- **Cross-Functional Collaboration:** Encourage collaboration between product, marketing, sales, and customer service teams. Sharing insights across departments fosters a holistic approach to product enhancements.
- **Feedback Loop:** Establish a feedback loop that keeps customers informed about how their feedback is influencing product development. This helps customers feel valued and promotes brand loyalty.

Case Studies

Several companies illustrate the successful integration of customer feedback:

- **Dropbox:** Initially started as a simple file storage application, user feedback helped Dropbox add features like file sharing and collaboration tools, making it more comprehensive for teams.
- **Lego:** The company encourages fans to submit ideas for new products. They review and potentially produce popular suggestions, creating a loyal community of creators.

Conclusion

Integrating customer feedback into product development creates opportunities for innovation that resonate with actual market needs. When organizations actively seek, analyze, and implement user insights, they enhance the likelihood of successful product launches and satisfied customers.

3. Encouraging Team Creativity and Collaboration

Understanding Creativity in Teams

Creativity is the lifeblood of innovation, and fostering it in teams involves creating an environment where diverse minds can collaborate freely. This leads to unique solutions and valuable insights that drive business growth.

Creating a Supportive Environment

To stimulate creativity, organizations must foster a supportive environment:

- **Encourage Open Communication:** Promote an atmosphere where team members feel safe expressing their ideas without fear of judgment.
- **Diverse Teams:** Bringing together individuals with varied backgrounds, expertise, and experiences cultivates diverse perspectives, enhancing creativity.
- **Physical and Virtual Spaces:** Design workspaces that promote collaboration, such as open layouts or breakout areas. For remote teams, utilize collaborative online tools and platforms.

Strategies to Boost Creativity

Several strategies can be employed to enhance team creativity:

- **Brainstorming Sessions:** Schedule regular brainstorming sessions where team members can freely share ideas. Utilize techniques such as mind mapping or the "Six Thinking Hats" approach to stimulate diverse discussions.
- **Improv Workshops:** Conducting improvisation workshops can help teams think on their feet and adapt to unexpected challenges. These exercises promote spontaneity and innovation.
- **Creative Challenges:** Organize hackathons or design sprints where teams tackle real problems within a time constraint. This encourages focus and rapid idea generation.
- **Encourage Side Projects:** Allow team members to pursue passion projects related to their work. This autonomy can lead to serendipitous innovations that benefit the organization.

Building Effective Collaboration

Effective collaboration is essential for the expression and combination of ideas:

- **Clear Goals and Roles:** Clearly define the objectives of team projects and the individual roles required to achieve them. This ensures accountability while preserving room for creative input.
- **Regular Check-Ins:** Schedule frequent team meetings to discuss ideas, provide support, and share progress. These interactions maintain momentum and facilitate idea sharing.
- **Collaboration Tools:** Utilize project management and communication tools (e.g., Slack, Trello, Zoom) to streamline processes and ensure everyone is aligned.

Celebrating Creativity

Recognizing and celebrating creative accomplishments encourages ongoing efforts in innovation:

- **Recognition Programs:** Implement awards or recognition programs that celebrate innovative ideas and team accomplishments, inspiring others to contribute creatively.
- **Showcasing Innovations:** Create platforms for teams to present their creative solutions to a larger audience within the organization, fostering a sense of pride and encouraging a culture of innovation.

Conclusion

Encouraging team creativity and collaboration is imperative for innovation. By nurturing an open, diverse, and supportive environment, organizations can unlock the collective potential of their teams and drive meaningful advancements.

4. Keeping Pace with Industry Trends and Disruptions

The Necessity of Staying Informed

In today's rapidly changing marketplace, startups must remain vigilant about emerging trends and disruptions. Staying informed enhances strategic decision-making and fuels innovation.

Researching Industry Trends

Several methodologies can be implemented to research and monitor industry trends effectively:

- **Market Research Reports:** Regularly consult industry reports and research studies that provide insights into market dynamics, customer behavior, and emerging technologies.
- **Follow Thought Leaders:** Engage with industry leaders, influencers, and analysts through social media or newsletters. Their insights can guide you on relevant trends impacting your sector.
- **Networking:** Attend industry conferences, webinars, and local meetups to connect with peers. These interactions often reveal insights into emerging trends and best practices.

Analyzing Disruptive Threats

Disruptive threats can emerge from unconventional competitors, technological advancements, or changes in consumer behavior:

- **Technology Watch:** Dedicate resources to closely monitor technological advancements that could disrupt your industry.
- **Competitive Intelligence:** Analyze competitors to identify their strategies, innovations, and market positioning. Understanding their movements can provide foresight into potential disruptive threats.
- **Consumer Behavior Analytics:** Leverage data analytics to track shifts in consumer needs and preferences. Being responsive to these changes gives businesses a competitive edge.

Strategic Adaptation

As organizations identify trends and disruptions, adapting strategies is critical:

- **Be Agile:** Embrace agile methodologies that allow teams to pivot quickly in response to shifts or disruptions. Being responsive can redefine competitive advantages.
- **Innovation Hub:** Create an in-house innovation lab or team dedicated to exploring new ideas, products, or service concepts based on emerging trends.
- **Evaluate Business Model:** Regularly assess your business model for relevance. Are there new revenue streams to explore? Are there inefficiencies that can be addressed?

Case Studies in Adaptation

History provides several vivid examples of businesses that successfully navigated industry trends:

- **Netflix:** Originally a DVD rental service, Netflix seamlessly transitioned to streaming media and revolutionized content consumption based on technological advancements.
- **Kodak:** Once a leader in photography, Kodak failed to adapt quickly to the digital imaging revolution. Its story illustrates the importance of vigilance to industry changes.

Conclusion

Keeping pace with industry trends requires proactive effort and vigilance. By conducting thorough research, remaining agile, and strategically adapting business practices, organizations can position themselves to thrive amidst constant change.

5. Embracing Failures as Learning Opportunities

Understanding the Value of Failure

Failure is often perceived negatively in the business context. However, embracing failure is fundamental to innovation. It presents valuable lessons that pave the way for future successes.

Creating a Safe Space for Failure

To encourage a culture that embraces failure, organizations must create a safe environment:

- **Normalize Failure:** Encourage team members to share their failures openly. When teams see failure as a part of the journey, they are more likely to experiment and innovate without fear.
- **De-stigmatize Failure:** Counter the fear of repercussions from failure. Emphasize learning and growth rather than blame, ensuring individuals feel secure taking calculated risks.

Learning from Failures

Reflecting on failures provides insights that prompt growth:

- **Conduct Post-Mortem Analyses:** After a project fails, hold meetings to analyze what went wrong. Identify specific areas for improvement and document key takeaways.
- **Encouraging Iteration:** Use lessons gleaned from failures to iterate on processes and products. This feedback loop enhances product development and performance.
- **Sharing Stories:** Create platforms where team members can share their failure stories and the lessons learned. This promotes a culture of learning from one another.

Resilience in Innovation

The path to innovation is often paved with setbacks:

- **Develop Resiliency:** Encourage individuals and teams to develop resiliency. Resilient teams bounce back stronger from failures and view challenges as opportunities for growth.
- **Set Realistic Metrics:** Realistic expectations set teams up for success. Understanding that not every venture will succeed helps in managing disappointment while maintaining motivation.

Successful Companies That Embrace Failure

Several organizations exemplify the concept of learning from failure effectively:

- **Amazon:** The company embraces failure as part of its culture and encourages innovation. Projects like the Amazon Fire Phone were failures, but they provide insights for future innovations.
- **Spotify:** Frequently runs experiments that may not succeed but ultimately help refine their streaming service, leading to innovations like customizable playlists.

Conclusion

Embracing failure as a learning opportunity fosters a culture of innovation within organizations. By normalizing failure and encouraging reflective learning, companies can build resilience and drive continuous improvement in their endeavors.

This detailed exploration of the topics related to **"The Road to Innovation"** offers insights and actionable strategies for startup leaders seeking to create a culture of innovation in their organizations. By foster teamwork, encouraging creativity, staying informed, and learning from failure, companies can navigate the complexities of the modern marketplace and turn their visionary ideas into reality.

CHAPTER SIXTEEN

Envisioning the Future

Envisioning the Future

1. Setting Long-Term Goals and Vision for Growth

Setting long-term goals is crucial for any startup that aims to thrive and adapt to changing market conditions and customer preferences. It establishes a clear direction, provides motivation, and allows for the measurement of progress over time. Here are some key aspects to consider:

Defining a Clear Vision: The first step in setting long-term goals is to define your vision. A strong vision statement outlines what you want your business to achieve in the future. This statement should be inspiring, realistic, and a guiding light for all levels of the organization.

SMART Goals: When establishing goals, consider the SMART criteria: Specific, Measurable, Achievable, Relevant, and Time-bound. This structure provides clarity and ensures your goals are actionable. For instance, instead of saying "Increase revenue," a SMART goal would be "Increase revenue by 25% in the next fiscal year by expanding to two new markets."

Resources and Skills Assessment: Evaluate the resources currently at your disposal. Understanding your team's strengths and weaknesses helps in setting realistic long-term goals. It's also vital to assess your financial resources, technology, and any other assets that will contribute to achieving your goals.

Periodic Review and Adjustment: Long-term goals should be fluid rather than fixed. The business environment evolves rapidly, and as new challenges and opportunities arise, it's essential to periodically review and, if necessary, adjust your goals. Regular reviews foster an adaptive mindset and help ensure that the business remains aligned with its vision.

Employee Involvement: Involve your employees in the goal-setting process. Their insights can provide valuable perspectives and assist in fostering a culture of commitment and alignment. When employees understand the long-term goals and their role in achieving them, it enhances engagement and productivity.

2. The Role of Sustainability in Modern Business Practices

In today's marketplace, sustainability has moved from being a niche consideration to a fundamental aspect of business operations. Companies that embrace sustainable practices not only contribute positively to the environment but also improve their brand reputation and drive growth.

Corporate Responsibility: Sustainability is not just about environmental impact; it encompasses social and economic dimensions as well. Businesses should adopt a holistic approach to corporate responsibility, ensuring that their practices contribute positively to society, from fair labor practices to community engagement.

Sustainable Supply Chains: Implement sustainable practices throughout the supply chain to reduce environmental footprints. This includes sourcing materials from sustainable suppliers, reducing waste, and minimizing transportation emissions. A transparent supply chain enhances consumer trust and can open avenues for new partnerships.

Innovation in Sustainability: Innovating sustainable products or business models can differentiate a company from its competitors. For example, using biodegradable materials or developing energy-efficient products can attract a growing consumer segment committed to sustainable living.

Regulatory Compliance and Risk Mitigation: Regulatory bodies worldwide are increasingly imposing stricter environmental regulations. By prioritizing sustainability, businesses can mitigate risks associated with non-compliance while potentially benefiting from government incentives.

Market Demand: Consumers are becoming more environmentally conscious, and many prefer to support brands with robust sustainability practices. By aligning business practices with consumer values, companies can enhance customer loyalty and attract a broader audience, providing a competitive edge.

3. Leveraging Emerging Technologies for Future Success

Technology is a powerful catalyst for innovation and growth. Startups that harness emerging technologies can optimize operations, enhance customer experiences, and create entirely new business models.

Artificial Intelligence and Machine Learning: AI and machine learning algorithms can analyze data faster and more accurately than traditional methods, providing valuable insights into customer behavior and market trends. Implementing these technologies can improve decision-making and increase operational efficiency.

Internet of Things (IoT): IoT technology allows devices to communicate and share data, creating smarter solutions across industries. For startups, leveraging IoT can improve operational transparency, optimize resource utilization, and enhance products or services, leading to improved customer satisfaction.

Blockchain for Transparency and Security: Blockchain technology can revolutionize how businesses operate by increasing transparency and security in transactions. Startups in supply chain management, finance, and health care can benefit from its decentralized nature, ensuring data integrity and building trust with customers.

Remote Collaboration Tools: The rise of remote work necessitates the adoption of collaboration technologies that facilitate communication and project management. Utilizing cloud-based tools not only boosts productivity but also attracts top talent irrespective of geographical constraints.

Data Analytics for Strategic Insights: Advanced data analytics enable startups to gather and analyze vast amounts of data to make informed decisions. By leveraging predictive analytics, businesses can identify market opportunities and customer preferences, shaping offerings that resonate with their target audience.

4. The Importance of Agility in Business Strategy

In a rapidly changing business landscape, agility is imperative for startups to respond effectively to trends, challenges, and opportunities. An agile business strategy allows for flexibility and quick adaptation, fostering innovation and resilience.

Iterative Development: Adopt an iterative approach to product development where feedback loops are integral to the process. By releasing minimum viable products (MVPs) and iterating based on real customer feedback, startups can enhance products according to market demand quickly.

Cross-Functional Teams: Encouraging collaboration among cross-functional teams can break down silos and increase agility. Diverse teams are better equipped to approach problems creatively and make decisions quickly, enhancing the overall responsiveness of the organization.

Scenario Planning: Incorporate scenario planning into your strategic toolkit. By considering various future scenarios, startups can prepare for unexpected challenges, ensuring they remain proactive rather than reactive to changes in the market.

Change Management Processes: Having robust change management processes in place allows startups to adapt their strategies smoothly. This includes clear communication of change, training and support for employees, and a culture that welcomes adaptive thinking.

Continuous Learning Culture: Foster a culture that values continuous learning and supports experimentation. Encouraging employees to pursue training, attend workshops, and share knowledge promotes a landscape of innovation and responsiveness to industry shifts.

5. Preparing for the Next Generation of Entrepreneurs

As the business landscape evolves, preparing for the next generation of entrepreneurs is vital. These new leaders will face unique challenges and opportunities that differ from those of their predecessors.

Mentorship Programs: Establish mentorship programs that connect experienced entrepreneurs with emerging leaders. This transfer of knowledge can offer invaluable insights and practical tips for navigating challenges and building successful businesses.

Embracing Diversity: Encouraging diverse voices in entrepreneurship leads to broader perspectives, innovative ideas, and solutions that resonate with wider audiences. Initiatives aiming to support underrepresented groups can cultivate a thriving culture in entrepreneurship.

Digital Literacy and Skills Development: Provide resources and training focused on digital skills. The next generation of entrepreneurs must be proficient in using technology to manage operations, market products, and analyze data effectively.

Encouraging Risk-Taking and Resilience: Create an environment that values calculated risk-taking and resilience over perfection. Understanding that failure is often part of the entrepreneurial journey encourages young entrepreneurs to learn from setbacks and continue pursuing their visions.

Networking Opportunities: Facilitate networking opportunities for young entrepreneurs to connect with each other, established businesses, and investors. Building these relationships early on can provide support, collaboration, and potential funding opportunities crucial to growth.

Conclusion

Envisioning the future is an essential aspect of entrepreneurship. By setting long-term goals, emphasizing sustainability, leveraging technology, maintaining agility, and nurturing the next generation of entrepreneurs, startups can create a resilient foundation for success. Each of these factors plays a critical role in navigating the ever-changing business landscape, ensuring not just survival, but thriving in a competitive marketplace. The entrepreneurial journey is as much about dreaming and launching as it is about growing and preparing for the future. As visionaries, entrepreneurs should embrace change and opportunities, staying committed to innovation and progress for themselves and the generations to come.

This breakdown aims to provide a robust foundation for each topic, establishing a comprehensive understanding of the key themes within the chapter "Envisioning the Future." Each section addresses the importance of forward-thinking strategies necessary for sustainable entrepreneurial success.

About Author

AUTHOR - SHIKHAR SINGH